Before You Study Theology

Before You Study Theology

Donald G. Luck

WIPF & STOCK · Eugene, Oregon

BEFORE YOU STUDY THEOLOGY

Copyright © 2021 Donald G. Luck. All rights reserved. Except for brief quotations in critical publications or reviews, no part of this book may be reproduced in any manner without prior written permission from the publisher. Write: Permissions, Wipf and Stock Publishers, 199 W. 8th Ave., Suite 3, Eugene, OR 97401.

Previously published as Why Study Theology by Chalice Press, 1999.
This edition is a scanned facsimile of the original edition published in 1999.

Wipf & Stock
An Imprint of Wipf and Stock Publishers
199 W. 8th Ave., Suite 3
Eugene, OR 97401

www.wipfandstock.com

PAPERBACK ISBN: 978-1-6667-3109-5
HARDCOVER ISBN: 978-1-6667-2324-3
EBOOK ISBN: 978-1-6667-2325-0

SEPTEMBER 13, 2021

To my children
Lindsay, Geoffrey, and Michael

Contents

Preface	ix
1. Why Complicate Things?	1
"All We Need Is the Bible"	2
"We Should Simply Trust the Leading of the Spirit"	8
Summary	12
2. Again, Why Complicate Things?	17
"We Should Focus on Committed Discipleship"	17
"God Calls for Faith, Not Doubt"	20
Summary	25
3. Why All This Intellectualizing?	27
"Theology Is Too Abstract"	27
"Theology Is Just Theory"	31
"Theology Doesn't Produce Clear-Cut Results"	34
"Theology Is Intimidating"	37
Summary	43
4. The Importance of Theology	47
Personal Benefits	47
A Communal Reference Point	49
The Need for a Theologically Aware Laity	51
The Christian Rabbi	56
The Resident Theologian	59
Summary	63

5. The Goals of Theology	65
Theology as a Rational Discipline	66
General Purposes	72
Systematic Theology	78
Summary	85
6. Constructing Theology	89
The Local "Architect/Contractor"	89
Building Materials	95
Developing a Blueprint	109
Beyond the Labels "Liberal" and "Conservative"	111
Summary	116
7. Developing Skills in Critical Thinking	121
A Point of Departure	123
The Challenge to Reach Out	126
Learning to Make Judgments and Cases	132
Summary	139
Postscript	145

Preface

This book is not designed to be yet another "Introduction to Theology." There are many such books on the market, and they are very helpful in laying out the task.[1] I will touch on many of the same concerns as they do, but my aim is more preliminary than that. In theological circles, one encounters the term *prolegomena*. The term comes from the Greek and means "the things that get said beforehand." In other words, prolegomena refer to the preliminary remarks that need to be made before one gets involved in the subject. Introductions to theology do that. But if that's the case, then what I am presenting are some prolegomena even to these prolegomena. I hope they will prove helpful, particularly to persons who are suspicious of theology or who are resistant to it. These would include both laypersons who are interested but cautious and also students in undergraduate religion classes and persons in seminary who are studying theology not out of genuine interest but because it is an academic requirement.

There are a number of reasons why persons, including some who enter seminary, think that the discipline of theology is unnecessary. In fact, for some, theology can even seem to be an obstacle to the childlike faith Jesus commends. Some persons assume that Christian faith has resources and claims that make theology superfluous. Others question the value of the form theology takes, namely, abstract thinking that examines ideas and constructs theories.

---

[1] A list of such resources will be found at the end of chapter 6.

These are very significant objections and need to be faced before we can look at what theology involves and how it is carried out. To be up front about it, in the process of working through these objections we will actually be doing some theologizing. We will try to think carefully about implications of the Christian faith. And we will be unearthing unconscious assumptions, raising critical questions, and presenting rationally coherent arguments.

In addition, increasingly persons who start their study of theology at a theological seminary have not had traditional preparation. The church itself developed the study of the liberal arts in the Middle Ages in order to prepare persons for theological study and ordination. It is not just that traditional preparation introduced persons to an understanding of Western history, which has been integrally connected to the development of the Christian church. It's more fundamental than that. A basic effect of liberal arts is to train persons to work with abstractions, become critical thinkers, and recognize the importance of constructing and testing theories. It also quietly communicates the insight that ideas are real—something that most people don't realize. In this way, a traditional liberal arts education prepares persons to study theology. But fewer and fewer students of theology in seminary have such preparation. That makes necessary some prolegomena before the usual prolegomena.

In looking at these issues, I will be addressing readers with a general—though not constant—assumption that, like most of those who make the effort to study Christian theology, they are Christians themselves. At the same time, I realize there will be students who are studying Christian theology in an undergraduate setting and using this book who are not necessarily Christians or even participants in *any* religious community. And that is completely appropriate. Christian theology is an interesting discipline. Even though it lies at the heart of the Christian community, it is possible for persons on the periphery of the church and even outright nonbelievers to study it. This is much the same as the possibility of a Christian engaging in Islamic or Buddhist studies or becoming knowledgeable about atheistic critiques of religion. Therefore, because I will tend to speak as a

Christian to other Christians, I beg your indulgence if you cannot personally identify with my implicit and explicit references to "we." At the same time, it should be possible for a student of theology who is not a believing Christian to follow my lines of argument and see how they reflect the way that Christian theologians approach their task.

The same kind of "fine-tuning" is asked on the part of those readers who are not studying theology with the goal of seeking ordination or commissioning in various forms of ministry or in the priesthood. Not only is it possible to study theology apart from ordination, it is also possible to teach it without being ordained. To be sure, the numbers of professional theologians who are not ordained is a minority, but their numbers have continued to increase in recent years. But because theology is integral to the ordained office, special attention will be given to those connections. Consequently, although I will occasionally have special words for those who are beginning their studies of theology either in undergraduate or seminary settings with ordained ministry in mind, those who have other interests should be able to profitably "overhear" what is said.

I have another public acknowledgment to make. The use of the first and second person is highly discouraged in academic writing. Authors should avoid referring to themselves as such. Do you note? I just used the academically correct form, rather than saying, "I shouldn't refer to myself directly as such." The reasons are not simply stylistic. The custom is meant to convey the understanding that the author is conveying something more than personal opinion or emotionally colored views. Instead, scholarly work is just that—the result of careful research, theorizing, and rational justification. There is much to be said for this style of writing and the concern that underlies it. But on many occasions I will set aside that academic caution and will directly address you, the reader, as such at times.

A good part of the reason is pedagogical. It has been my experience that students of theology usually approach the subject from a very personal point of view. Somewhere they carry deep, emotionally colored convictions, even if it is the conviction that organized religion is hopelessly irrelevant, irrational, or worse. I know from personal experience and observation of students that emotional and personal factors are always at work. Sometimes they contribute to an individual's resistance to theology. In that case, ignoring them doesn't gain anything. That is why at times I will address some of these underlying concerns and write in a more personal and direct style. This doesn't fit the usual patterns of scholarly writing and study, but it does, I believe, address persons who are beginning a journey of theological study.

Religious concerns, convictions, questions, and affirmations usually have the weight of seriousness about them. To be quite open about it, a central goal of theology is to help you learn to develop measures of healthy intellectual detachment and discipline. Doing so shouldn't mean ignoring or abandoning the emotional and spiritual dimensions of religious concern. But it does mean cultivating as much care and objectivity in thinking about religious and theological matters as possible.

Let's turn now to the first cluster of "the things that get said beforehand" by noting a number of objections to theology, starting with those that have what we might call a "religious" character. But before we push on, let me first say a few words of thanks to a number of people who supported this writing project. First, to the Board of Directors of Trinity Lutheran Seminary for providing the time needed by granting me sabbatical leave from my teaching responsibilities; then to the encouragement of President Dennis A. Anderson and the invaluable support and helpfulness of my friend and colleague, Mark Allan Powell. My colleague Walter Bouman, Robert Schreiter of the Catholic Theological Union in Chicago, and Paul Knitter of Xavier University all provided valuable responses to an early version of the manuscript. And I could not have managed without Nona Jensen's computer literacy and transcriptions of early copy. I also deeply appreciate the lively interest of my editor, Jon L. Berquist of Chalice Press, in "an introduction to introductions to theology." But most of all I would like to thank my students at Trinity Lutheran Seminary and Concordia College, Moorhead, Minnesota, who helped me see the need for this book and work out ways to address that need.

1

Why Complicate Things?

Even though students take up the task of theology, it doesn't mean they do so willingly. Many times it is the result of having to fulfill a requirement in the curriculum of a college, university, or seminary, not personal interest or enthusiasm. And perhaps that is the very reason you are reading this book right now. It's a requirement. Let me see if I can meet some of you where you are by identifying and speaking to some objections to theology that I have encountered in my teaching career. And see if I provide a helpful response to some or all of these objections. Even if my responses do not necessarily eliminate these objections, see if they can to a degree moderate some of them. If so, I will not only be talking *about* theology, I will be demonstrating how to "do" theology. I will be presenting arguments, making cases, and seeing if what I am pointing to doesn't make *sense*. That is central to the theological task.

When I say "I" here, it refers to more than private opinion. It will reflect my dependence on and participation in a community of disciplined inquiry and reflection that is active now and has been in the past. This is also part of the theological task. More will be said about this later.

Let's turn now to some common objections that people have to theology.

"All We Need Is the Bible"

Without question the Bible has a special place in the Christian community, especially for Protestants, who, from the time of the Reformation, have appealed to it as the fundamental authority for life and thought. Millions seek inspiration and guidance from its pages. And even theologians themselves appeal to scripture to substantiate their arguments. Scripture is the bedrock on which the church builds its life and witness, since it is the closest we can get to the experiences that were understood to be communications of the presence, nature, and will of God. Central to Christians are the life and ministry of Jesus and the history of the people of Israel that established the background and living context in which Jesus functioned. Our access to these experiences is through literature that reflects or directly points to them.

Therefore, many are persuaded that the enterprise of theology is unnecessary. People need only the scriptures and a believing heart and they will understand clearly God's will for their lives and God's word to the world. For example, Martin Luther made statements to the effect that the most humble peasant reading the Bible can more clearly understand what the gospel is than the learned university professors whom the papacy quoted.

But it's not that simple. In the first place, Luther himself was a learned university professor. He was a student of scripture who made it a point to read these ancient writings in the original Hebrew and Greek in order to understand their meaning better. And he soon discovered that he had deep and sometimes bitter disagreements with others who equally appealed to scripture as the authority for their arguments. These included those who cited the Bible in denying the validity of infant baptism and those who argued for the possibility of "Christianizing" the political realm, views that differed from Luther's.

The point is, no one—university professor or peasant or we—ever reads the Bible in a vacuum. And because we do not, we don't always agree on what it is saying. The reading of scripture is as much shaped by the one who reads as it is by what is read. We bring ourselves, our assumptions, our interests, even our prejudices to what we read.

That's why there is widespread acknowledgment that persons can find backing for almost any opinion within the pages of the Bible. We have to admit the possibility that while we believe we are reading something *out of* scripture, we can actually be reading something *into* it. The technical terms for these two alternatives are *exegesis* and *eisegesis*, respectively.[1]

If the church is going to appeal to scriptural authority, it needs to use the best possible resources for understanding the two assemblages of various writings that have been collectively called "the book" (*biblos* in Greek) or "the writings" (*scriptura* in Latin). Accordingly, biblical scholars work hard at analyzing these writings in terms of both their historical and cultural settings and their features as forms of literature. But even this helpful and necessary scholarly work doesn't deal with all the issues.

Let's think for a moment of how Christians unconsciously evaluate and prioritize biblical materials. They do this so automatically that it slips by their notice, but it shouldn't. They need to stop and ask themselves what sorts of criteria operate for them when they respond to various passages of scripture as they do.

Even fundamentalists who claim the entire Bible is not only *inspired* by God but actually *infallible*—that is, without error—don't actually operate as if every segment of scripture is of equal value. In a lengthy section of Exodus (chapters 25–40), for example, there are detailed descriptions of the materials and patterns for the ark and tabernacle used in Israel's exodus wanderings. In only a few verses of chapter 5 of Amos, on the other hand, the prophet cites God's insistence that sacred ceremonies and offerings are unimportant. What God prefers, Amos argues, is commitment to justice and integrity. Almost everyone would probably assume that the latter reference, though much briefer, is more

---

[1] You will discover that most theological terms are derived from Latin or, as in this case, Greek. Note the list of theological dictionaries found at the end of this chapter. They will help you understand such terminology as well as many other things about the study of theology.

important than the former. But why? What are readers presupposing?

Selective emphasis and prioritizing is always at work, even among those who believe they are centrally dependent on scripture. To cite Luther again as an example, even though he insisted that scripture is *the* foundation of Christian life and faith, it's instructive to note that he dismissed entire books of the Bible because he thought they had little value. He mused that the Bible is the manger in which the Christ child is to be found, and Christians are to worship not the Bible but the Christ it contains. Perhaps he had this metaphor in mind when he called the Epistle of James an "epistle of straw," since to his way of thinking it doesn't understand the gospel of grace as well as the writings of Paul. And he said that the book of Esther could well be left out of the Bible, since it doesn't even mention God once! And as for the book of Revelation, he argued, its cryptic language lends itself to the hare-brained interpretations of crackpots, so we would have been better off following the advice of the early Eastern church in keeping it out of the canon.

We all have implicit criteria that we use to evaluate and prioritize particular segments of scripture. To follow up on Luther as an example, his central criterion was clear. The scriptures, he said, are meant to "drive us toward Christ," either in repentance or in radical trust. Furthermore, he argued, such a standard is not arbitrary, since it reflects Paul's basic distinction between relation to God "under the law" and relation to God "through the gospel." This is not to argue that Luther's views are undisputed, but it is to say that even someone who insisted that scripture *alone* has final authority (*sola scriptura*) had to make arguments outside of scripture. Therefore, even if we might not agree with Luther's treatment of scripture and the criteria he used, we should at least recognize that he was above board about his standards of judgment and that he provided arguments for their validity. And so should everyone else. But to do that is to do theology.

Our unconscious assumptions also guide our interpretation of biblical materials. Consider the fact that both the Hebrew and Christian scriptures assume the givenness of slavery. Nowhere is there an outright repudiation of this institution. In fact, in several places (Eph. 6:5–9; Col. 3:20 ff; Titus 2:9) slaves are encouraged to show obedience to those who own them. What should we make of that? Or what about the regulations governing the sexual treatment of women captured in battle (Deut. 21:10–14)? Do we consider them God's word for us? However we respond, we need to recognize that our interpretation is implicitly appealing to authorities and lines of argument beyond the pages of the Bible itself. Doing this is equivalent to doing theology.

We usually aren't aware of these assumptions and appeals, but they shape the reading of scripture profoundly. Being careful and faithful interpreters means "coming clean" and being held theologically accountable for the ways we read the Bible. We might be uncomfortable having to identify and justify our assumptions. And if we are not sure of ourselves, we may become defensive and pound pulpits or attack the Christian identity of those who disagree with or question us. But our assumptions are exactly the issue.

They certainly are relevant when we have to reconcile what seem to be outright internal contradictions. In Psalm 139, for example, the psalmist cries out: "O that you would kill the wicked, O God,…Do I not hate those who hate you, O Lord? And do I not loathe those who rise up against you? I hate them with perfect hatred; I count them my enemies"(vv. 19, 21–22). These words are biblical, but it is hard for us to believe they would be found on the lips of the crucified Jesus. And they clash with the insistence in 1 John 4:20 that loving God and hating another person are totally incompatible. But harmonizing varying elements of scripture means we have to rely on arguments that go beyond the scriptures themselves. Such argumentation amounts to doing theology.

There is also a problem reconciling certain elements of the Bible with what seem to be external contradictions, that is, with the growing bodies of knowledge about the natural world and human nature that emerge from the extensive investigations of science. Because of its central appeal to the authority of scripture, Protestant theology has been split more by this issue than by any other over the last two centuries. It remains a battlefield, for example, for Christians who oppose the teaching of evolution in public schools because they believe it contradicts the clear teachings of the first two chapters of Genesis. But even Christians who are not fundamentalists have had to figure out what to do with these biblical accounts and how to relate them to the claims of science. Our assumptions are not self-evident or uncontested. Once we are challenged to explain and justify them, we realize we have to do some very careful thinking and explaining. And this is precisely what *doing theology* means.

This need for thoughtful examination, reflection, and explanation becomes even more obvious once we begin to examine scripture closely. Careful reading unearths hidden problems. For example, look at Acts 2. New Testament scholars believe that the author was depending on very early materials here. Let's bracket out for a moment other New Testament materials, later Christian notions, and our automatic tendency to homogenize everything in the Bible as if everything were saying the same thing. If we then look carefully at what this text is saying on its own, what we find is rather startling. In verses 24 and 32, Jesus' resurrection is spoken of in the passive voice. Jesus did not "rise" but "was raised." Moreover, a distinction is made between Jesus and God—and it is God, not Jesus, who is the active agent. Yet later Christian literature in the New Testament itself and in materials like the Apostles' and Nicene Creeds speak of the Christ who "rose" on the third day—active voice. What do we make of this passive voice, particularly if it is early material?

The puzzling problems deepen when we look closely at verse 36. Here it is asserted that in raising Jesus from the dead, God "has *made* him both Lord and Messiah" (italics added). Now, that is quite extraordinary. Long-standing Christian tradition has assumed that Jesus is the Christ from the moment he is conceived. But the material in Acts 2 presents a different picture. Jesus was faithful to God and because of that obedience was put to death. But God vindicated him by raising him from the dead, and this act exalted him and made him "both Lord and Messiah." Again, the point is, whatever we make of these issues, we have to do some careful thinking and explaining. That amounts to doing theology.

Finally, the need for theology becomes all the more pressing when the church has to discover what being faithful to Christ means in changing historical and cultural situations. How do we interpret scripture in regard to pressing contemporary issues? We've already noted that many biblical passages can be cited to support slavery. Accordingly, nineteenth-century abolitionists had to do some very careful theologizing and in the process also had to give reasons why they challenged the biblically grounded arguments of Christians who supported slavery.

Today, churches face challenges to traditional notions about the nature and place of women, not only in society but also in the church itself. The traditions of the social subordination of women and the specific exclusion of women from public leadership in the church appear to have strong biblical support, just as slavery did. Examining these issues today in the light of scripture is also causing scripture to be examined in the light of these issues. Some want to set aside biblical passages that restrict the role of women as historically and culturally bound; others believe they are timeless. But regardless, proponents of either position have to go beyond the Bible itself and provide cogent theological arguments.[2]

Yes, the Bible remains a central resource for the Christian community, and it has a fundamental authority. However, for that very reason it makes theology necessary. If we really want to listen to the scriptures and let them have authority in the church, then we need to approach them carefully. We must understand them for what they are and make neither more nor less of them than is warranted. We must let them speak on their own terms, not on the terms of our unjustified and questionable and eventually arbitrary

---

[2]The impact of theology responsive to the contemporary women's movement is known as feminist theology. Comments and resources that provide an introduction to feminist theology will be provided later.

assumptions. We need to engage in careful and informed thinking.

"We Should Simply Trust the Leading of the Spirit"

There is another objection to theology that needs careful examination precisely because there is an important element of truth in it. It is the belief that more than anything else Christians should seek to have Jesus live in their hearts. Focusing on straightening out ideas in their heads, it is argued, is the wrong emphasis.

That is a valid caution. Life in God is not fundamentally a system of belief at all, much less a rational examination and explanation of belief. Rather, it is trust and love and commitment. The scriptures attest to that over and over again, and so do the broad reaches of Christian experience. The fact is, most of the time we are more moved by the lives of Christian saints than we are by the arguments of Christian theologians. And believing Christians probably are more shaped by the worshipping and serving life of Christian congregations than they are by formal instruction.

Christian identity is centered in recognizing who God is and what God's meaning and will for our lives are. It is supremely true that we are claimed by nothing less than God's Spirit, which transforms and directs our life in the world. The only problem is, what "spirit" is God's Spirit?

Wide varieties of claims are made as to what it is and isn't. Sometimes it has been identified with sheer nonsense and embarrassing miscalculation. At other times there have been tragic, destructive results. Over the course of Christian history, all sorts of movements, which the wider wisdom of the time or the hindsight of subsequent years have shown to be mistaken, have claimed to be led by God's Spirit.

Moved by the Spirit, Francis of Assisi is said to have preached to the birds. There's something charming about that, even if it doesn't necessarily help us discover the Spirit in our own lives. But we need to remember that, claiming to be moved by the Spirit, church officials called for military crusades against Muslims and burned people at the stake.

As Paul cautions, we need to test the spirits. We need God's grace to help us discern what is truly the expression of the Holy Spirit moving among God's people and the currents of history and what isn't. We have to evaluate the enthusiasms and commitments that claim Christians. Part of that testing includes noticing their fruits. What results are there? And are these coherent with earlier Christian experience and especially with the life, the Spirit, that moved Jesus?

But testing also entails making careful investigations and equally careful arguments. That's what occurred in the Confessing Church movement in Germany earlier in this century, as it challenged widespread enthusiasm in the churches for the outlook and spirit of the Nazis. It's hard for us to believe here and now that such an alien "spirit" could seize so many pastors and church-going people, but it did. At the time, the horrors of war had not been felt and the concentration camps had not been built. But the spirit that built them was already evident. Against that enthusiasm, the members of Confessing Church mustered careful and vigorous theological arguments. They were a minority then and were swept aside, but their bold witness and equally careful arguments encouraged thousands of people to resist Nazi policies and ideas.

This event in our own time demonstrates that one of the most important tests of what is and isn't "of the Spirit" is that of intelligibility. Paul himself refers to that test when writing about what today we call "speaking in tongues." He notes that he himself had this special ability, which he believed was a gift of God's Spirit. But, he argues, "in church I would rather speak five words with my mind, in order to instruct others also, than ten thousand words in a tongue" (1 Cor. 14:19). A sense of personal commitment and deep religious enthusiasm are not enough.

Life in the Spirit may be more than theology, but it must make sense. It must be rationally coherent. If we abandon that criterion, then we open the door to all sorts of aberrations like the Nazi theories of racial superiority and inferiority, or like the countless numbers of sects that keep springing up to claim that we are living in "the end times." The fact is, we make rationally based judgments about emotional claims all the time.

A number of years ago, while teaching in the religion department of a college, I had a student who experienced mental illness. By participating in a counseling program and by taking medication, he was able to remain in school. But unfortunately he came under the influence of a charismatic religious community who convinced him his condition was caused by demon possession. That possession, these people argued, was perpetuated by his willingness to trust the secular medical community rather than God. Under their direction he stopped seeing his therapist, ceased his medication, and underwent "exorcism" at the hands of the group's leader.

Only a short while later, one bitterly cold winter night, he was reading the Bible in order to discern the leading of the Spirit. He came across Paul's words "walk in the Spirit" (Gal. 5:16), as they are translated in the King James Version. Feeling that to be God's directive, he set out on foot in near-zero weather for his girlfriend's home some eighty miles distant, singing hymns and stopping at farm homes along the way in order to tell their inhabitants that the end of the world was near at hand. Police finally picked him up and brought him to the psychiatric ward of a hospital, where he began a slow, tortuous process back to some emotional stability.

It's a tragic story and certainly an obvious case of confusion about what the Holy Spirit means. But the clear lesson is that life in the Spirit is not irrational, and it does not contradict sound human understanding about how we and the world are put together. To pit life in the Spirit against theology is dangerous. It leaves us open to confusing the true nature of the Spirit with all sorts of nonsense, superstition, prejudice, and even, as this story demonstrates, mental illness.

Life in the Spirit must be coherent not with some special Christian version of rationality but with a reasonableness that can be recognized by all human beings. This should be no surprise. Christians believe that God is the author of the world and all that is in it, and that includes human intelligence and understanding. Just as you cannot find life in Christ merely by thinking carefully or by studying theology, so you are foolish to believe that it ignores or contradicts our natural capacities for thinking rationally. Thomas Aquinas, the great theologian of the Middle Ages, put it this way: "Grace does not destroy nature but rather fulfills it." God's unique self-communication does not contradict human knowledge of reality.

It is the task of theology to investigate just where and how the coherence between the truth of Christ and the truth of human rationality can be discovered. In doing this, the care and discipline that Christians are expected to exercise is not meant to be arid or bloodless. Theology is not detached thinking; it is believing thinking. It is "faith seeking understanding," as another medieval theologian, Anselm of Canterbury, put it.

At heart it should be a form of love. Yes, love. Living theology wants to express what it means to love God not only with all one's heart and with all one's soul and with all one's strength but also with all one's mind (see Mt. 22:37; Mk. 12:30; Lk. 10:27). Sometimes that is hard to see, but it really is theology's deepest motivation.

Reading Thomas Aquinas' great work *Summa Theologiae* is like reading an exercise in abstract philosophical argument. He sets up theses and then examines arguments for, then those against, and finally draws rationally coherent conclusions. He cites Aristotle more than he does scripture. And his commitment to logic is dispassionate. But at the time he was writing his theology, Thomas was having mystical visions in the chapel. And one day he had a vision of Christ appear and say to him about this rationally rigorous book, "Thomas, you have written well of me." That's because for Thomas, loving the truth is loving God; serving the cause of discovering the intelligibility of Christian faith is serving Christ.

Theology is not meant to displace life in the Spirit. Rather, it is meant to grow out of it and to clarify what that life means. When theology is arid and dull and irrelevant, it no longer serves the Spirit or is a vehicle for the Spirit. But then it no longer serves the cause of intelligibility either. Seeking to make sense of the faith entails discerning how it speaks to and intersects with the scope and depth of human experience and insight. Such commitment enables theology to serve God and express love for God. And it ends up creating exciting theology!

Summary

- We never read the Bible in a vacuum. Consequently, we need to be conscious and reflective about the presuppositions that determine how we interpret it, prioritize its contents, and sort out questions about it.

- No one escapes using the Bible without looking for some guidance or authority from outside its pages, even if this is done unconsciously. We need to do this honestly and openly and be held accountable for the appeals we make.

- All of this is essential if we are to let the Bible speak on its own terms instead of having our reading merely reflect the views we project into it. By doing careful and informed theology, we respect the Bible's authority by examining our own presuppositions.

- It's true that it is God's Spirit and not theology that is foundational for our life in Christ. But eventually we need to be clear about what this Spirit is and isn't. There are misguided and even destructive enthusiasms and commitments.

- To pit the Spirit against theology is dangerous. It leaves the door open to all sorts of nonsense, prejudice, and emotionally ill claims. Scripture associates God's Spirit with intelligibility.

- At rock bottom, theology is not bloodless intellectualizing. It is living out the commitment to love God with all one's mind. Living theology grows out of life in the Spirit.

For Further Reading and Reflection

It is important that you begin to become familiar with the technical language of theology. An invaluable resource is a theological dictionary. I suggest that you buy one right now and use it consistently, particularly in the early phases of your theological study.

Theological dictionaries are never neutral. Not only the definitions that are provided but even the topics that are selected always reflect the theological commitments and biases of the editors and authors. I will make some notes about that factor below. Some titles you might want to consider are:

Douglas, J. D., et al. *Concise Dictionary of the Christian Tradition: Doctrine, Liturgy, History.* Grand Rapids: Zondervan, 1989. A resource prepared by and meant for fundamentalist and traditionalist Protestants.

Elwell, Walter A. *A Concise Dictionary of Evangelical Theology.* Grand Rapids: Baker Books, 1996. As the title suggests, the author is a person shaped by evangelical conservative Protestant theology.

Hardon, John A. *A Pocket Catholic Dictionary.* Garden City, N.Y.: Doubleday, 1985. The title says it all.

Komonchak, Joseph, Mary Collins, and Dermot A. Lane, eds. *The New Dictionary of Theology.* Collegeville, Minn.: Liturgical Press, 1987. Lengthy treatments of theological topics relevant to Roman Catholic theology by several authors.

McKim, Donald K. *Westminster Dictionary of Theological Terms.* Louisville: Westminster John Knox Press, 1996. The author provides brief definitions of nearly six thousand entries and provides a helpful resource with a concluding listing of other theological dictionaries and encyclopedias under the title "Works Consulted."

Musser, Donald W., and Joseph L. Price, eds. *A New Handbook of Christian Theology.* Nashville: Abingdon Press, 1992. Extensive treatment of a select number of major topics by mainstream Protestant and Roman Catholic authors. A special feature is an initial guide titled "Routes for Reading," which notes relevant entries in the handbook for seventeen basic theological issues.

O'Collins, Gerald, and Edward G. Farrugia. *A Concise Dictionary of Theology.* New York/Mahwah, N.J.: Paulist Press, 1991. A compact dictionary by two authors covering topics especially relevant to post-Vatican II Roman Catholic theology.

Russell, Letty M., and J. Shannon Clarkson, eds. *Dictionary of Feminist Theologies.* Louisville: Westminster John Knox Press, 1996. As the use of the plural in the title indicates, feminist theology encompasses a variety of perspectives. The authors of entries explain more than terminology, and they provide an introduction to this important new development in theology.

Two very helpful resources that are out of print but that are worth tracking down in used book stores or libraries are:

Halvorson, Marvin, and Arthur Cohen, eds. *A Handbook of Christian Theology.* Cleveland: World Publishing, 1958. Extensive treatment of one hundred major topics by leading mainstream Protestant theologians at mid-century.

Harvey, Van. *A Handbook of Theological Terms.* New York: Macmillan, 1964. Almost three hundred fifty major topics treated by a Methodist theologian.

Because scripture is so basic to Christian theology and even more so to Christian worship and devotional life, students should make extra effort to become acquainted with some of the assumptions, goals, and patterns of academic biblical scholarship.

Broadly speaking, the biblical scholarship that shapes the life of mainstream Protestant, evangelical conservative Protestant, and Roman Catholic communities is increasingly an interchangeable and shared enterprise. It is not surprising, for example, to find Protestant scholars who are members of the Catholic Biblical Association or Roman Catholics who are leading figures in the Society of Biblical Literature, which has Protestant roots. In fact, there is a full mix of people in the academic arena, including, surprising at it may seem, New Testament scholars who are Jewish and biblical scholars who are not participants in any religious community. The fundamental criterion is not whether or not a scholar's views are "orthodox" from any particular perspective, but rather if they are intellectually defensible.

The patterns of scholarly inquiry into the collection of writings known collectively as "the Bible" have the umbrella term *biblical criticism.* The term *criticism* does not have the negative connotations it has in popular usage but indicates scholarly analysis. It indicates a careful examination of the writings contained in the Bible, which is an integral part of the work of attempting to understand the wider world through disciplined reflection. Donald McKim defines biblical criticism as "the study and investigation of biblical writings through many means to understand elements such as their backgrounds, forms, history, authorship, audience, message, language, circumstances, and relation to other biblical writings."[3] He also goes on to give brief definitions of most of the sub-disciplines of biblical study.[4]

Even when people don't necessarily recognize the need to integrate scripture with so-called secular knowledge, they are constantly doing so, even in half-conscious and confused ways. For example, one can often hear church people making the argument that the six "days" of creation mentioned in the first chapter of Genesis really refer to indeterminate periods of time, not six successive twenty-four hour days. But the text says no such thing.

This raises some interesting questions. Where do people get the warrant for reading the words of scripture in ways that the text itself does not suggest? What would prompt people to interpret the text this way? Is this anything more than a purely arbitrary point of view? Theology consciously aims to get beyond mere opinion or ungrounded assertions. As with this text in Genesis or with any and all religious assertions, it aims at having us become self-conscious and responsible for our views. It asks us to become aware of our assumptions, put them on the table, examine them carefully, and see if they can be justified. The process can seem intimidating, but it also enables us to discover an understanding of religious matters that can have measures of intellectual grounding and vindication.

---

[3]*Westminster Dictionary of Theological Terms* (Louisville: Westminster John Knox Press, 1996), 67.

[4]Ibid., 67–68. The relevance of biblical scholarship to the discipline of constructive theology will be examined briefly in chapter 6.

2

Again, Why Complicate Things?

"We Should Focus on Committed Discipleship"

There is an objection to theology that is closely related to the one we just examined. What distinguishes it is its stress on the importance of committed action. In part this reflects the deep suspicion in American culture that often there is too much thinking and not enough doing. We are a nation of doers. It's no accident that inventors like Thomas Alva Edison and the Wright brothers are popular heroes. They weren't very educated, but they were creative people. Thinking has value for us primarily when it is put to good practical use.

Therefore it is not surprising that in such an atmosphere, theology seems fairly superfluous. For Americans, religious identity is usually connected to compassionate, ethical activity. It's as if we are saying, "If you want to know what persons believe, watch what they do."

Again, we need to recognize that this is a valid and helpful observation. Jesus himself said, "Not everyone who says to me 'Lord, Lord' will enter the kingdom of heaven, but only the one who does the will of my Father in heaven" (Mt. 7:21). And in one of the most dramatic of Jesus' parables, he depicts pagans (which is to say Gentiles) being judged on the basis of loving and serving God in terms of what they have done to the lowliest persons (Mt. 25:31–46). The implication of Jesus' parable is that God ultimately focuses on what persons have done, how they have been disposed toward others, not their formal belief and certainly not any conscious theology.

But the fact is that our actions and reactions are always guided by our basic beliefs. In pointing to "beliefs" I am not thinking of abstract religious doctrines, although I do believe the teachings of churches are highly influential in shaping people's lives. Instead, I am talking about the fundamental outlook we have toward life, which we use to evaluate and make sense of our experience. Like our assumptions about the Bible, this fundamental outlook is not something we are conscious of very often. It's more like a pair of glasses that sits on our nose. We may not be aware of them, but we don't see anything else without them.

A sociologist has said that every one of us walks around with "a basic reality kit." That kit is composed of all those hardly conscious assumptions we have about how the world is put together, why it works the way it does, and what helps to make sense of events. What's interesting about basic reality kits is that we all take them for granted and assume everybody sees things as we do. Yet basic reality kits are not uniform. They differ from one culture or era to another and are constantly modified by changing experience

Our fundamental beliefs are associated with our basic reality kits. But they also include our basic values, our deepest hopes, the loyalties that shape what we care about and guide what we do, and the interpretative frameworks of meaning into which we place our experience. We might call these beliefs our "basic meaning kit."

On July 19, 1989, the United Airlines DC-10 flight from Denver to Chicago cartwheeled and broke into fragments as it made an emergency landing at Sioux City, Iowa. Many passengers were killed but a number survived. Days later, reporters from *Life* magazine spoke with some of these survivors and asked them to remember what had happened and if they had been changed by it. The resulting article is interesting reading. Objectively, all those interviewed went through the same incident. But existentially they experienced differing events because of the filters of belief and interpretation through which this shared happening passed.

Some saw their survival as a miracle, as the direct intervention of God. Others, including both an agnostic and a Christian, said that in light of the dead babies and young mothers such notions of divine intervention were repulsive. Some indicated that the experience would make them much more attentive to religious practice, but others believed that sort of response would be hypocritical. Life's priorities had shifted for some, but others reported that life went on very much as it had before this traumatic event. Interestingly, several Christians, a Buddhist, and an atheist all reported that their basic religious views were confirmed and deepened by the experience.

Behind all of these differing reactions lie the fundamental beliefs of these different people—their assumptions for interpreting experience, their notions about what is meaningful and important, and their convictions about life and death and self and world. It isn't often that they or we are conscious of these religious beliefs. And even such a traumatic happening as this crash did not cause all the survivors to look consciously or deeply into themselves. But the reactions of each and every person were reflection's of his or her "basic meaning kit."

A number of moves must be made from these implicit outlooks to the discipline of theology. Perhaps the most central goal of the church's preaching and teaching ministries, its worshiping life, and its counseling is to influence the basic outlooks of people. The goal is to make Christ real and present, so that in seeing him believers see themselves, each other, their world, and the flow of their lives differently. Sometimes being busy and active is actually a way to avoid looking at life deeply or allowing basic assumptions to be challenged.

Daniel Berrigan once said that the message of the Buddha was: "Don't just do something! Stand there." It helps not to be busy all the time, to take time out, to become aware of what makes us tick at the most fundamental levels. Life-shaping events, particularly traumatic and tragic ones, can prompt us to do just that. And the church tries to encourage this process at special junctures in people's lives—such as when they become Christian converts or enter into adult church membership or seek ordination. The goal isn't merely for them to become conscious of their underlying beliefs, but to have them be shaped by the guidance of its official teaching. To do this is to engage in theology.

Certainly theological reflection is no substitute for engaged Christian action. But because our implicit beliefs shape our identities and our responses to life, they are the key to the way we act. Taking stock of our life assumptions, doing informed and careful theology, can reshape our beliefs. Sometimes such theological reflection turns out to be the prelude to deepened discipleship, not an escape from it.

"God Calls for Faith, Not Doubt"

Another major "religious" objection to theology is one that is widespread. People are nervous about the radical questioning that theology encourages. Beginning students in theology soon discover that all sorts of widespread ideas and opinions they thought to be official church teaching are challenged and even denied by those who make theology their life's work. Walking into a classroom where they assume their beliefs will be strengthened, they can discover that some of them are being undermined. The academic study of theology seems to encourage doubt.

This anxiety is often tied to a suspicion that theologians exercise a great deal of spiritual pride. By challenging, questioning, and raising doubts, they appear to place their own human intelligence above the truth of the Bible and the cherished beliefs of the past. Theology seems linked to human presumption and arrogance. In the Fourth Gospel, Jesus rebukes Thomas for his doubt and disbelief. It would seem he would equally rebuke the intellectual and spiritual pride of constantly questioning, doubt-inducing theologians.

I have a confession to make. As a young theologian fresh from graduate school teaching in a college setting, I sometimes fell into the sin of intellectual pride and found that I enjoyed pulling the theological rug out from underneath my students. But, thank God, it didn't take long for life to help me outgrow this sophomoric practice. For one thing, I found that my real targets were the remnants of my own naïveté, which continued to embarrass me. For another, I soon discovered as a teacher that I wasn't helping my students grow, something I wanted more than anything else. I quickly abandoned that style along with my supposition that I ought to shape my courses as if they were scaled-down versions of my graduate school education.

So it is true that human arrogance and spiritual pride can infect theology. But it is also true that they can equally be found in people's dismissal of theology. Just sense the spiritual attitude that lies behind the bumper sticker that growls, "God said it! I believe it! That settles it!"

A little theological clarification can help us at this point. We need to examine our working definitions of *faith* and *doubt*. Some long-standing traditions in the Christian community define faith in a way that seems to exclude the right to question scripture, church tradition, widespread beliefs and practices, or (especially) what we learned at our mother's knee. *Faith* is often associated with notions of "submission." In this view, our faith is our willingness to put ourselves under God's guidance and authority.

Another viewpoint understands *faith* to mean the willingness to believe something to be true even though there are few or no reasons for doing so. "You've got to take that on faith," we hear people say. Add to this the use of the term *faith* to refer to the traditional teachings of the church, as in the phrase "professing the Catholic faith." Together these definitions encourage the widespread assumption that we should unquestioningly subscribe to traditional teachings and believe them to be true even though there is little or no evidence for them. Our *doubt* is our arrogant refusal to do so.

But if we look closely at the Hebrew and Christian scriptures, we will see that *faith* has a different primary meaning. It means willingness to trust God. The opposite of such faith is not intellectual doubt or the unwillingness to submit to the formal authority of the church or the Bible. Instead it is the spiritual condition of mistrust. *Faith* implies the willingness to live in the world in a state of radical risk and openness because one surrenders control of life—even one's life of faith—to God. The focus of faith, then, is not teachings or ideas, not the bible or church doctrine, but rather the living God.[1]

Unfortunately we are tempted again and again to compromise this posture of radical trust in God and instead place our basic trust in things we can get a handle on. We even end up having faith in our own faith. For some of us this means priding ourselves on our orthodoxy. For others of us it means priding ourselves on our own sense of psychological confidence. And for others still it means pride in our commitment to faithful discipleship.

However, all of these religious exercises are rivals to trusting *God*, because in each case the object of faith is something that has to do with ourselves and that lies within our grasp. But God is *never* in our grasp. That is part of the very definition of what makes God God. That's what it means to say that God is "infinite," that is, not (*in*) limited (*finitus*). As one theologian put it, God may be *at* hand—that is, God may be present to us—but God is never *in* hand. That is why the first commandment, which stresses the supremacy of God, is followed by the second, which cautions against the creation of idols. In saying this, the Hebrew scriptures are not simply criticizing the practice of making statues. They are cautioning against confusing God with anything that is part and parcel of the finite world. Consequently, the prophets had highly critical things to say about the religious practices of their day. People were confusing them and their involvement with them with trusting and serving God alone.

---

[1] A very thorough but theologically advanced examination of this understanding of faith is found in Paul Tillich, *The Dynamics of Faith* (New York: Harper & Row, 1957).

The implication of all this is that our trust in God actually gives us encouragement to doubt and question. Because we do not have faith in our own faith, we can allow ourselves to be led more deeply into the truth. We need to admit as Paul does that our knowledge and proclamation are partial at best (1 Cor. 13:9). No human being can ever say that she or he possesses the truth. At best we can say we are possessed *by* it.

Faith *does* mean submission to God. But that implies our submission to a truth *larger* than ourselves. Tennyson once wrote, "There lives more faith in honest doubt than in half the creeds."[2] Honest doubt means the willingness to humbly place oneself under the truth. Honest questioning is submission. Ultimately, God is the author of all truth, just as God is the author of all that is. Therefore, as the great theologians of the past argued, whenever persons honestly seek the truth, they are responding to God. This is true even if, like Socrates, they dare to question cherished traditions. An unbeliever who is a dedicated disciple of the truth is more truly God's disciple than a Christian who wants the security of absolute certainty and is afraid of asking questions.

Alan Watts has some helpful insight into the dynamic and mobile character of faith. It is always on the move. That is why honest questioning may be the prelude to deeper religious affirmation. He writes:

> Most of us believe in order to feel secure, in order to make our individual lives seem valuable and meaningful. Belief has thus become an attempt to hang on to life, to grasp and keep it for one's own. But you cannot understand life and its mysteries as long as you try to grasp it. Indeed, you cannot grasp it, just as you cannot walk off with a river in a bucket. If you try to capture running water in a bucket, it is clear you do not understand it and that you will always be disappointed, for in the bucket the water does not run. To "have" running water you must let

---

[2] Alfred Tennyson, *In Memoriam* (Oxford: Clarendon Press, 1982), xcvi.

go of it and let it run. The same is true of life and of God.[3]

This means, however, that the doubt that is coherent with faith is not a cynical or arrogant dismissal of the church's teaching. There are persons who are just as absolutist and cocksure of their atheism as there are others who have the same attitude in regard to their religious fervor. The real issue here is whether or not persons place themselves *over* or *under* the truth.

One implication is that we should not summarily dismiss the teachings of the past or the importance of the Bible. If we are truly disciples of the truth, we would be just plain foolish to ignore a wisdom and range of spiritual experience larger than our own. But faith in God does mean that we can dare to ask probing and difficult questions without feeling guilty or presumptuous. The very seriousness of our questioning is the evidence that we are asking God to lead us more deeply into the truth, the truth that in the final analysis is grounded in God alone.

There are important cautions about the limits of theology. But often these "religious" objections (as I have chosen to call them) rest on mistaken assumptions or draw unwarranted conclusions. I admit that in trying to understand and speak to these criticisms of theology I have actually engaged in doing some theology, which may seem to beg the question. In other words, I am using theology to defend theology. But it's important to note that in disagreeing, critics cannot avoid pursuing the equivalents of theological reflection and argument themselves.

Speaking for and to Christians, I would want to argue that the issue is not whether or not we should engage in theology. Instead, it's a question of whether or not we will do so in an informed and careful way.

But we still need to look closely at other objections to theology, ones that arise not so much within the church as within our culture. These are not simply objections to

---

[3] Alan W. Watts, *The Wisdom of Insecurity: A Message for an Age of Anxiety* (New York: Random House [Vintage Books], 1951).

theology as such, but to the sort of enterprise it is, namely, intellectualizing. So let's turn to what I call "cultural" objections next.

Summary

- The spirit of American activism tends to pit action against belief and make it more primary. But our basic beliefs shape how we look at life and how we respond to it. Our actions are guided by our beliefs.

- Traumatic events can sometimes connect us consciously with our basic beliefs about ourselves, life, the world, God. The church encourages us to become aware of our basic beliefs and wants them to be shaped by Christ. It does this by communicating how Christian theological tradition has already made these connections.

- Theology is never a substitute for engaged Christian action. But theology can help us take stock of our lives and reshape the way we live in the world. It can be the prelude to deepened discipleship.

- Sometimes we assume that faith excludes doubt. And sometimes we are nervous about asking questions about our Christian life. We can assume that persons who dare to question are prideful. But questioning need not contradict faith, and an unquestioning, unthinking attitude can itself be prideful.

- Often *faith* is identified with submission and unquestioning belief, but in scripture it fundamentally means trusting God. Such trust is constantly threatened by our hunger for security and a sense of control.

- Unlike having faith in our faith—that is, having confidence in our own orthodoxy, or sense of psychological certainty or commitment—trust in God encourages us to be open to the growth that can come through honest questioning.

- All questioning that really seeks the truth seeks God, whether it knows it or not. The unbeliever who is a disciple of the truth is more God's disciple than the Christian who wants absolute certainty and is afraid of questions.

For Further Reading and Reflection

After reading this chapter and thinking about what it says, what do you make of the argument that beliefs are more fundamental than actions? What implications might this have for American religious life, which is set in a culture fundamentally oriented to being practical? How do you respond to Berrigan's depiction of the Buddha's message ("Don't just do something; stand there!")?

3

Why All This Intellectualizing?

Just as there are objections to theology that reflect religious concerns, so there are others that are suspicious of the sort of enterprise it is. As we've already noted, ours is a "hands on" culture. Americans respect the down to earth, the practical, anything that can demonstrate its effectiveness. We are doubtful, however, about the value of abstract analysis. Therefore, like all other forms of intellectualizing, theology does not seem to have much evident value for most of us. Our culture prejudices us against theology.

"Theology Is Too Abstract"

Because Americans question how much value should be attached to ideas, they are suspicious of persons who are fascinated with abstract thinking about things. Sitting around theorizing is one thing, actually being involved in the world of action is another. To use the technical term, Americans tend to be *pragmatists*, that is, they tend to determine the meaning and truth of concepts and test their validity by their practical results.

Perhaps you know the fictional, humorous story of the four authors asked to write a book about elephants. The

Englishman turned out a leather-bound volume, complete with maps and illustrations, titled *The Elephant and the Rise of the British Empire*. The Frenchman's slim volume was called *Les Amours des Elèphantes* (*The Love Life of Elephants*), while the German, true to that culture's love of thorough investigation and analysis, produced a four-volume work, with innumerable indexes and footnotes, titled *Der Elefant: Eine Einleitung* (*The Elephant: An Introduction*). (As you may already know, Germans produce a great deal of theology.) The American's book, on the other hand, had the title *Bigger and Better Elephants!*

Unlike intellectuals, who by their very nature are interested in working with ideas, most Americans prefer practical problems. Theorizing seems an empty exercise. So it is not surprising that Americans stereotype intellectuals as persons who are so caught up in books and theories and ideas that they can't seem to balance a checking account or wear matching socks. And sometimes this can come close to the truth.

I still remember a college friend telling me about meeting one of our classics professors deep in thought, strolling across the campus with a milk carton in his hand. Greeting him, my friend asked why he was carrying it along. The professor looked at the milk carton in astonishment, thanked my friend, and hurried back home. Apparently he had been so lost in thought that he had unthinkingly put the travel alarm he always placed on his classroom desk in the refrigerator that morning and took along the milk carton instead.

But as remote or comical as fussing with ideas may seem, ideas are real and are very important. They change the world. In other words, even by pragmatic standards, ideas are real because they have practical consequences.

Consider our tendency to contrast the abstract interests of intellectuals with down to earth common sense. But ironically, what we assume today as common sense was hardly that for the average person in the Middle Ages. At that time, for example, "common sense" knew that the world was flat, that disease was spread by the night air and by bathing, that kings had the right to rule over people because they were placed there by God, and that certain persons were witches who could cast evil spells on others. We have come a long way from such earlier "common sense." And the reason we have a totally different set of assumptions about these and other matters is due in large measure to thoughtful and sometimes very brave persons who dared to question givens, carry on intellectual inquiry, and come up with different operating ideas. And they did this despite widespread popular indifference and even outright opposition.

Look closely at our belief that all human beings are created equal and have the right to determine who it is that governs them. Such an assertion hardly describes how human beings have been viewed and how governments have functioned down through the centuries. On the contrary, the actual political affairs of almost all societies operated very differently until more and more persons began to entertain novel thoughts about life. Eventually a group of intellectuals, meeting in Philadelphia in the latter part of the eighteenth century, used these and related ideas to *invent*, to *think up* a nation and its government. Ideas are real. The reshaping of life depends on them.

We express our humanness in everything from literature and film to systems of government and the way we tell the story of our own culture. We even express it in organizing a group of citizens to challenge the local school system or in the narratives persons tell in order to explain why they are divorced. Intellectualizing is the attempt to get inside everything human beings create and do in order to understand what is going on. Intellectualizing abstracts from the concrete through our capacity to understand, to form ideas. And the goal is to give us life-shaping insight. Intellectual abstraction can waste time and ideas can be wedded to nonsense, but thinking in a disciplined and informed way is necessary in order for us to gain new and wise perspectives.

Therefore, just because something seems abstract does not mean it is unreal. Christians insist, for example, that God is real. Yet God is not evident in the way in which most realities are. A factory worker once told an industrial chaplain that when he hears the word *coffee* he can identify it with something concrete. He can mentally smell its aroma, see the steam rising from the cup, and anticipate its taste. But when he hears the word *God* it means nothing because it is too abstract.

Certainly we would want to say that God is not simply an idea. But in order to understand what the word *God* means, we have to deal with it at the level of ideas. We have to abstract from Christian references to *God* and from activities that claim to be responses to God in order to understand what is being referred to. Only through such abstraction can we then begin to identify what God's reality is and how it is related to and different from the reality of everything else—including a cup of coffee.

Those who have had a liberal arts education or have been trained in disciplines like theoretical physics have been introduced to this practice of thinking abstractly. But more and more persons entering theological study today have either a limited background in thinking and arguing abstractly or have none at all. That is not to fault anybody's educational program. In many cases, students bring other experience and insight that can help them in theological study and, for those whose study is part of their path to ordination, in ministry. But it does require them to learn new skills.[1]

Undergraduate education is not the only factor. Not everyone has a natural inclination or a natural ability to work this way. Some discover more readily than others that ideas are real and that theories have consequences. This enables them to "catch on to" how to do theology more quickly. Given the fact that churches usually insist on competency in theology for those seeking ordination, this may seem to be unfair to those who don't have these abilities. But churches also look for basic proficiency in other areas like counseling, administration, worship leadership, public speaking, and simply relating well to other people. This variety of necessary competencies can sometimes balance things out. Persons who have little background or few natural gifts in abstract thinking will have to work harder at learning to think theologically.

---

[1]This issue will be taken up in chapter 6.

But they may be more naturally gifted in other areas. At the same time, intellectually oriented persons may have to work harder at skills other than theology.

The point is that in order to do theology persons need to discover the reality, the power, and the excitement of ideas. Without that discovery, theology will never come alive for them. The key here is to realize that the debates that go on and the analyses that are presented provide us with deeper insight into the meaning of our life in God. Theology does this by abstracting elements of the concrete activity of the Christian community and bringing them into the realm of ideas. Then, having gained clarity in this realm, it moves back with its understanding to shape the activity of the community. In this way, theology parallels the activity of liberal arts study, which aims to discover insight into the business of being human in order to humanize individuals and societies.

Theology tries to be aware of what we can profitably understand about the business of being human, which is unearthed by intellectual analysis of our culture and by the disciplines of what have been called *the human sciences* such as psychology, sociology, and political analysis. It then pursues an equally careful intellectual analysis of Christian faith in terms of its truth claims, its self-understanding, and the meaning of its convictions and commitments. In this way, it can potentially see how the business of being human intersects with what we might call the business of being a believing Christian. It is by abstracting and working with ideas that these two very different arenas can be brought together constructively. This leads us to consider a related objection to theology.

"Theology Is Just Theory"

Our pragmatic culture is not kindly disposed toward theories. We often hear the comment, "Well, it might sound good in theory, but it doesn't work out in practice." Like Sergeant Joe Friday on the old TV program *Dragnet*, we prefer "just the facts, ma'am." However, if theories don't line up with "the facts," with the way things are, then we need a better theory, rather than no theory at all. And sometimes we can't deal with the facts or even know what they are until we find a relevant and fruitful theory.

A faculty colleague once had to have his stereo system repaired, but when he took the receiver in, the repairman said that he couldn't fix it because he couldn't find a schematic inside the set that diagrammed the circuitry. So my friend took the receiver to another colleague who taught in the physics department, explained the problem, and asked if he could sketch out a schematic. "Of course," he replied. Now armed with the drawing, my colleague returned to the shop and had the stereo repaired. The reason the physicist could sketch out the schematic while the repairman couldn't is because the physicist knew all the relevant theories. He could figure out how the set in front of him was put together while the hands-on repairman could not. Theories are mental maps, and they are useful in enabling us to get around in the concrete world.

Theories also enable us to discover what "the facts" are. Theories don't simply help us sort out what we already know. They can actually generate discoveries. Einstein's theory of relativity theorized that the gravitational pull of bodies should bend light. It wasn't until a number of years later that experiments demonstrated that this is exactly what in fact happens. And the reason the experiments were devised in the first place was to test the theory.

The same holds true in theology. Theology proceeds by way of theory construction. The ideas that are abstracted from Christian sources—church life, scripture, the deep convictions of persons thought to be wise, and the like—are woven together in carefully thought-through and argued theories. These theories in turn can have a dramatic impact on the life of the church.

Take, for example, the decision of many churches in the latter part of this century to ordain women. This practice runs totally counter to almost twenty centuries of tradition. What happened? In the first place, questions and arguments raised in the secular arena began to spill over into the life of the Christian community. Within our culture, people began to challenge traditional ideas about women. They engaged in "consciousness-raising," questioning whether these ideas were true and whether the social structures they supported were justified. Reigning theories were examined and found wanting and were replaced with new ones.

These theories had their intellectual counterparts in the churches. In other words, they stimulated theological analysis. The results are interesting. Not only have these theories, these theological arguments, convinced many churches to reverse ancient tradition, they have stimulated New Testament scholars to look more closely at the Christian scriptures. The results parallel those of Einstein's theory about gravity and light.

Sensitized by feminist theorizing, New Testament scholars now find evidence that the earliest Christian community accepted leadership by women as well as by men. They also have discovered that Jesus had a radical openness to women unparalleled in his day. And they are fascinated with the fact that Paul names several women as leaders in the church, something known but skimmed over by earlier generations. These facts of early church life were undercut by later tradition and were overlooked by earlier scholars because of the unconscious, male-oriented assumptions of the culture. It has been the *theorizing* of feminist analysis that has enabled us to discover them.

So we can begin to see how important theory is. The Greek root of the word is the same as for the word *theater*. Originally a theater was an outdoor structure, usually cut into the side of a hill and having curved seats looking down on a stage. From those seats, spectators had a vantage point, they gained a perspective, on the action of the play. That's what a theory does. It gives us a vantage point from which to view and evaluate what is going on. It gives us perspective. Theology is the theorizing carried on by the Christian community in order to create a helpful perspective on what the church is and does and believes.

Clergy today, for example, are expected to fill many roles and perform many tasks. Very often, however, little question is raised about the prioritizing or even the appropriateness of these responsibilities. Many—including ordained persons themselves—see the primary role of clergy as caregivers. But is that a primary task? Should clergy be more concerned about reaching out to hurting and needy persons than any other Christian? Is it even justified as a professional role at all? Are clergy best qualified to do so, or can other persons—including "secular" types such as therapists or social workers—actually be more informed and effective? Sorting through issues like this calls for the crafting of a perspective, a theory, a *theology* of ministry.

Perhaps no place is the need for clergy to carry out the discipline of theorizing more evident than in the task of preaching. We shall look at this issue more fully later.[2] Suffice it to say here that in order for preaching to come alive and address the living issues facing individuals and society as a whole, the preacher needs the capacity to think theologically. Only the broad perspective that theology provides can enable the preacher to understand how the witness of scripture and the wider Christian tradition intersects with what is going on in the depths of human personalities, human relationships, and social, national, and global life. Only then is there a chance that a living Word will be spoken that God wants addressed to God's people and to the world. We have already noted how theorizing about the nature and status of women has caused church practice to change. Today there are even broader consequences, as theologians begin to recognize the domination of the church's life and thought by males and see how the value of the alternative experience of women can give the church a new perspective on its life and witness. Because perspective is valuable, theory is indispensable.

"Theology Doesn't Produce Clear-Cut Results"

Another reason why we may be initially put off by theology is our frustration with the fact that its work is never done. For all the theorizing that goes on, theologians never seem to speak a final word, and for all the arguments that are advanced, counter arguments inevitably spring up.

---

[2]See "The Resident Theologian" in chapter 4.

All this is true. But isn't this also true for politics? The reason political arguments and policies shift is because national and global circumstances change. And sometimes solutions to particular problems raise new ones. Before World War II most Republicans were isolationists, but after the war they argued vigorously for an American military presence around the world. Liberal Democrats wanted American troops to be brought home from Vietnam, but later some wanted U.S. military intervention in Bosnia. In the past, persons argued that a national welfare program was needed in order to help the radically poor in the country. Now even some of its most liberal supporters believe that the present welfare program perpetuates poverty.

The fact that debate is never over and new forms of action are continually called for does not invalidate the debate and action of the past. We always think and act in specific circumstances using limited insight and being motivated by particular concerns. All of that is subject to change, and given the dynamic character of life, it eventually does. The same holds true for theology.

There is another parallel in the work of science. As much as we have come to know, we discover there is more to learn. In fact, major discoveries often open up entire fields of research that had not been anticipated. I remember coming across the ironic reflections of a British physicist who, as a young graduate student after World War I, was determined not to pursue any work that could possibly be used to support warfare. Consequently he avoided work in physics relevant to ballistics and instead settled on something seemingly militarily harmless and irrelevant—atomic physics. At the time he charted his professional career he had no way of knowing where such studies would lead. Knowledge keeps opening up new fields of inquiry and new problems.

The investigations and theorizing of science are never done. But that does not invalidate its past achievements any more than its future fruitfulness. And the same holds true for its method. Some biblical fundamentalists downplay the work of science because they do not like the way it seems to discredit what they believe are biblical assertions. Science is not to be respected, they argue, because its conclusions are never conclusive. The best science can do, they point out, is to spin out theories that cannot claim absolute certainty and that are always open to revision and replacement. In contrast they point to what they believe is a timeless and absolutely unquestionable Bible. But contrary to fundamentalist criticism, the fact that science's findings are not absolute and beyond continued questioning does not invalidate its methodology. Instead, it confirms it. *Because* science functions the way it does, it continues to discover the limits (not the total invalidity) of reigning theories and moves on to develop more adequate ones.

The same is true of Christian theology. Theologians—like preachers—are never asked to speak a final word on behalf of the church, but rather a faithful word, a word that is timely and helpful in specific contexts. Biblical scholars and church historians are constantly making new discoveries or proposing new theories to explain texts and events. The world of human inquiry keeps presenting the church with new information and insight into the nature of reality, especially the business of being human. The church finds itself in new historical situations and cultural contexts. Lessons from the church's past can be forgotten and have to be remembered all over again.

So it is not surprising that, like political debate and scientific investigation, theology's work is never done, and its results are never agreed on by everyone. But what matters is that the work be carried on, that differing points of view make careful cases and seek a hearing in the Christian community so that its belief and practice can be informed and helped.

Someone has said, "Life is a journey and not a destination." What is increasingly evident in our own day is that theology is being viewed in the same way. In the past it often seemed that theology dealt with a timeless truth that only had to be re-expressed again and again. This approach is called *theological repristination*. But actually theology has always embraced a great deal of historical dynamism, even if this dynamism was not consciously recognized until the last few centuries.

Contact with Arabs in the High Middle Ages introduced Europeans to large segments of Aristotle's writings that had been lost in the West. These ideas revolutionized Western philosophy and thereby created totally new theology. The cultural movement of the Renaissance stressed the importance of going back to original sources and understanding them in their original languages. The resulting study of scripture in Greek and Hebrew rather than in Latin translation had a profound effect on theology and helped create the Reformation. The rise of modern science and its challenges to Christian traditions stimulated radically new theological approaches. And today some argue that recognition of a global, pluralistic, and environmentally threatened world calls for new ways of thinking theologically. Right now, for example, there is interest in what sorts of new Christian theorizing will emerge from the churches that have been planted in African and Asian cultures and that increasingly feel at home there.

So the work of theology is never over. But that does not invalidate past results any more than it means that former arguments are a waste of time. The theological process itself is important, and its results, even though limited and subject to challenge, can have significant value. Sometimes the insights that were gained in the past turn out to have new relevance and a creative impact. Consequently, theology continues to interact with the historically and culturally new at the same time that it reminds itself of its past. All of this is to say, theology is a *process*.

"Theology Is Intimidating"

There is no doubt about the intimidating, overwhelming effect theology can have on the beginning reader. Its language can seem esoteric, its arguments complex, its working distinctions highly refined, and its practical usefulness obscure. Little wonder persons can be put off by it.

Sometimes theologians seem to argue about wispy and irrelevant topics. The great Renaissance scholar Erasmus is credited with criticizing the picky concerns and convoluted arguments of medieval scholastic theologians by charging that they argued about how many angels can dance on the head of a pin. Then along came the Lutheran and Calvinist scholastics in the seventeenth century. At times their writings seem just as bad—as if the former wondered whether angels danced at all and the latter asked whether, even if they were capable of doing so, they should be allowed to!

I believe that theologians need to admit that something like this often takes place today. The reasons lie in the wider intellectual climate. Theology has been under great pressure by the world of scholarship to demonstrate that it has intellectual respectability. The *academy*, as the world of disciplined study and argument is often called, has put great pressure on theologians, who have often been accused by secular intellectuals of dealing with little more than refined superstition or insupportable private notions based on nothing more than emotion.

Consequently, theology has made a strenuous defense of the intellectual vigor and integrity of Christian faith and life. But the result has many times been a crafting of theology more in conversation with the academy than with the believing community. This has tended to focus theology on concerns that lie far afield of where churchgoers live. Even more problematically, it has led some Christian scholars to stop being theologians, speaking for and to the church. Instead this challenge has encouraged them to analyze Christian faith and life as dispassionate academic scholars who are interested in religion in a professional and generic fashion. For some this switch in focus has been coextensive with their own loss of personal faith. The overall result is to distance certain segments of theological discourse from the life of the church and to pursue more and more academically specialized questions.

It will take a while, but eventually beginning students of theology can begin to recognize theology that is addressed primarily to the academy and that which is addressed primarily to the church. It will be easier to follow the latter. But they should not avoid intellectually demanding theological writing. In fact, from the earliest theology produced by the Christian community, theologians have believed that it was not only fruitful but also an expression of faithfulness to God to be accountable to both communities. In part it is because allowing ourselves to be stretched intellectually can be understood by Christians to be a form of discipleship, a placing of oneself under God as the foundation and goal of all understanding. But we all need to find our own pace. Above all we shouldn't let our very understandable frustration cause us to dismiss a particular work or even theology in general as worthless.

In the last chapter we will explore in detail some of the educational implications of developmental psychology. That discipline argues that the processes of intellectual growth, and the parallel processes of moral and religious growth, follow definite patterns. The overall direction of such growth is an increasing discovery and acceptance of the complex and constantly changing character of life. If we are presented with ideas that lie well beyond the range of what we already know and accept, we will be intimidated by them. In such a situation, the very certainty with which such ideas are presented will tend to anger us. That is because we can feel humiliated by the distance between ourselves and others who understand more than we do or who argue more successfully or knowledgeably than we. But these psychological studies have also shown that when we encounter ideas and values that are more nuanced than our own, but which we can come to understand by stretching our understanding just a bit, we can grow.

This means that part of the responsibility for effective communication rests with teachers and theologians. They should not "get too far out in front" of the given understanding of others they want to teach. They need to know their audience and "speak a word in season." But part of the responsibility is also the student's. As a student, you shouldn't expect every teacher or theologian to shape his or her presentations just to meet you where you are. Consequently, you need to be self-selecting in what you study and read. But as you do, you will need to be willing to let your understanding reach out from where it already is. And you need to admit that theology has a lot more to communicate than you will be able to grasp even by stretching yourself. At the same time, that is not an implicit criticism of you any more than it is a dismissal of what these theologians are saying.

Certainly this is true for any other subject. High school students beginning studies in physics can hardly expect themselves to understand doctoral lectures given at MIT. And it is no disparagement of them that they can't. Why should it be different for theology? Perhaps because theology affects the dearly held beliefs of people, they expect it should be otherwise. But even though theology is "believing thinking" as much as it is "thinking about believing," it still remains *thinking*. It is an academic subject even when pursued by the church for the sake of the church.

So the watchword is *patience*. Be patient with yourself as you carry out this path of study. Be patient when you can't understand what someone is saying, especially when your psyche starts to feel frustration and lashes out in angry dismissal. Help it to be understanding and realistic. Be patient with yourself for the time it takes for your understanding to expand. Give yourself the credit you deserve for the progress you do make and the attitude of openness and hard work you display.

And be patient with the obscure (to you) arguments you encounter in theological writings. It's usually the case that you are overhearing a conversation that has been going on for a long time. If you as an outsider heard persons talking about family matters, you would not be surprised that you didn't understand some, if not most, of the references they made. You wouldn't know what "Aunt Lena's usual attitude" meant. You wouldn't even know anything about Aunt Lena! And while you might be able to understand a bit of what they were saying, you would be totally in the dark if suddenly they switched to speaking in Slovak, the family language.

Much theology is like that. You are overhearing a conversation that has been going on for a long time and has many operating assumptions to it. Moreover, the language that is used is actually a highly technical language that not only comprises a special vocabulary but uses what looks like ordinary English in its own way. Theologians don't do this to be difficult. Sometimes, it is true, they have a tendency to slip into what almost seems to be a foreign language, one I call *academese*. It's a style of communication that tries to convey to other members of the academy the understanding that the author is highly knowledgeable about the issue and all related arguments, is widely read, cognizant of contrary views, and skilled at making arguments. As a theologian I plead guilty to the charge myself. And the results can be very disappointing. Too many theologians write for other theologians and too few for the widest possible audience.[3] But once again, have patience—and be understanding if your frame of reference seems to be ignored.

At the same time, realize that because it is a technical language, theology uses a kind of "shorthand." Once you come to understand the meaning of technical terms and once you know the background for points of view and their competing alternatives, you will understand passages and entire essays that used to confuse and frustrate you. Take, for example, the following sentence from Dutch theologian J. C. Hoekendijk:

> Ecclesiology cannot be more than a single paragraph from Christology (the *Messianic* dealings with the world) and a few sentences from eschatology (the Messianic dealings with the *World*).[4]

It would take several pages to spell out all that this one sentence is attempting to argue. Let me only call attention to a few of its more important elements. In the first place, it is a bold, even outrageous, statement, since it flies in the face of what many persons believe and what most theologians in the past have assumed. Hoekendijk is referring to *ecclesiology*. That's the technical term for the Christian understanding of the nature, meaning, and value of the church.

---

[3] One academically respected theologian consciously trying to interest laypersons in theology is John B. Cobb, Jr. See *Lay Theology* (St. Louis: Chalice Press, 1994) and *Becoming a Thinking Christian* (Nashville: Abingdon Press, 1993).

[4] J. C. Hoekendijk, *The Church Inside Out*, edited by L. A. Hoedemaker and Pieter Tijmes; translated by Isaac C. Rottenberg (Philadelphia: Westminster Press, 1964), 40.

Moreover, Hoekendijk is offering this not as a description of the way the church is but as a *prescription*. He means to argue how *God* sees the church and what the church is *meant* to be from that perspective.

What Hoekendijk is asserting is that concern for the church in and of itself is the wrong concern altogether. Anything having to do with the church as God intends it really belongs to two other considerations: christology and eschatology. Christology usually refers to understanding the person of Jesus Christ and how Christ is related both to the humanness he shares with us and to God's divinity. But Hoekendijk doesn't mean it simply in that traditional sense. He is referring to what Jesus Christ means to God's concern for the world and God's saving impact upon it. The christology he's referring to is not metaphysical, that is, it doesn't deal abstractly with human nature and the nature of the divine and how they intersect with each other in the person of Christ. Instead, his christology is existential, that is, it refers to the life-shaping meaning and spiritual impact that Christ has for the believing community and its individual members.

Eschatology traditionally refers to Christian understanding of the relation of salvation to time and more narrowly to the end of the world and eternal life. In the twentieth century, however, eschatology is viewed not as a separate topic but as an issue that intersects with the whole of Christian faith and life. And rather than referring to something in the future, eschatology is concerned with how God's presence and will intersect with the present. The promise of God's ultimate future profoundly shapes the way Christians live now. Consequently, concern about the church should be grounded in the final outcome of God's will, which will affect not simply the church but the entire human family, even the entire universe.

So what Hoekendijk is arguing is quite radical. A church concerned about itself is not the church God wants. God's saving presence and will are not focused on the church or restricted to the church. The next sentence makes Hoekendijk's argument clear: "The church is only the church to the extent that she lets herself be used as a part of God's dealings with the *oikoumene*." That last word is a New Testament Greek word that means the entire inhabited world. So God's saving will is focused not on the church but on the world, and the church's God-grounded meaning is realized when it mirrors the servant character of its Lord. The church exists not to be concerned about itself but solely to be like Christ in being responsive to God's saving will for the entire world. Perhaps now you will understand something of the implications of the title of the book from which this quote comes, *The Church Turned Inside Out*.

It has taken a great deal of explanation to unpack just one sentence of theology, and to do so in only a minimal way. But this illustration can help you understand how theology's technical language is a kind of shorthand and how the ongoing conversation of theology in our century provides the context for understanding how even traditional terms are used. So be patient—with yourself and with the material you read.

And be persistent. Like any other field of study, from car mechanics to quantum physics, theology requires persistent and solid work. But others before you have responded to this challenge, and they have not only managed, they have become personally involved. They have found that theology has changed them.

Summary

- The American disposition tends to dismiss dealing with ideas; but ideas are real and the reshaping of life depends on them. The same holds true for the church's understanding of its own faith and mission.

- By abstracting from the concrete, intellectuals are able to provide perspectives for reshaping and redirecting what human beings are, believe, and do. Theology is the exercise of this discipline on behalf of the church.

- Thinking abstractly is a skill that must be learned, and it is a natural inclination that comes more readily to some. But willingness to learn can enable all to discover more fully the reality, power, and excitement of ideas.

- Like politics, theology is never final, but the discussion itself guides concrete policy because it occurs in relationship to the dynamic character of life itself. Theology is called upon to speak a faithful—and timely—word, *not* a final one.

- Theology uses a technical language that requires getting used to, and sometimes this language is addressed more to the academy than to the church. Therefore, learn to be patient with yourself and the theologians you encounter in your study, appreciating your own efforts and the insights you gain from others.

For Further Reading and Reflection

Go back and review Hoekendijk's statement. Do you disagree with what he says, and if so, why do you respond this way? Do you find his assertion challenging, opening up an entirely new way to think about the church? Can you begin to see how taking this theological argument seriously might bring about changes in the ways in which congregations and the church as a whole might rethink their priorities and redeploy their energies?

The purpose of this example from Hoekendijk was to illustrate the argument that ideas are real and that they have the potential to change things. It also was designed to illustrate how abstracting a perspective by means of intellectual analysis enables us to enter back into the concrete flow of life in order to reshape it or even create something new. If Hoekendijk is right, what practical consequences can you see flowing out of his looking at the church in the way he does? What changes in church attitudes, priorities, and activities might occur?

My arguments for the value of theory are coherent with the American concern for the practical. My point is to demonstrate that intellectualizing and theorizing have important practical consequences.

This isn't the time to elaborate on arguments for the *inherent* value of theory, but I do want to signal at this point that there are rewards and claims for intellectual abstraction other than pragmatic ones. Something of this will be touched on later. But you ought to know that there have been theologians, for example, who have asserted that trying to understand the meaning of the Trinity has led them to states of mystical awe and worship. Knowing something about God is an end in and of itself. But the simple point remains: Ideas are real and the construction of Christian theory that is known as theology has value.

Before You Study Theology

4

The Importance of Theology

Personal Benefits

There are many potential personal benefits that can result from studying theology. Perhaps the most obvious is the opportunity to integrate our understanding of Christian faith and life with our understanding of the wider world in which we live. Discovering the bridges that can be built between the two can often have a deep spiritual and emotional effect on people. They find that they live less and less in two separate worlds, one reserved for their life in Christ and the other the public world they share in common with non-Christians.

The need to work at building such bridges is not a conscious or pressing one for great numbers of people. But some in the Christian community have become dissatisfied with their earlier unquestioning acceptance of their Christian upbringing. Sometimes this is due to jarring personal experiences that shake their understanding of the faith. Sometimes it is due to the impact of higher education that expands their sense of the wider world, a world in which the faith of earlier years seems out of place.

There are powerful turning points in personal histories. Major crises such as the tragic death of a loved one, the loss of a career or a marriage, the destructiveness of disease or war can often cause deep religious questioning. Certainly as people seek to work through these disruptive times they need the ministrations of pastoral care, prayer, and the support of the worshiping life of the community. But often they find themselves wanting intellectual support as well. They want deeper measures of understanding. Of course, those who provide ministry in such moments need to recognize that this questioning has a deeply emotional character. At the same time, these intense moments can encourage important theological reflection.

It is more often the case that persons become interested in theology because of the challenges to their childhood beliefs that advanced education poses. Unfortunately, not many opportunities present themselves to study theology in undergraduate settings because few schools have departments of theology or religion. But theology departments as well as campus pastors and Christian student centers adjacent to colleges and universities often prove to be resources for persons whose educational process raises theological questions for them.

It is my suspicion that a sizable percentage of church members, even if they do not represent the majority, are potentially open to far more theological study than they have experienced. My own experience in introducing persons to theology, not only in undergraduate and seminary classrooms but also in congregational educational programs, raises this suspicion for me time and again. Many don't even realize that the church even gives them permission to question and probe. And they are unaware of the theological resources that can be found to assist their intellectual growth in the faith. Again and again I hear people in all three of these settings acknowledge how helpful such study is for them. And again and again I hear them ask, "Why wasn't I introduced to this way of thinking before?"

As we have already noted, theological understanding is neither the whole of Christian discipleship nor its heart. But it is a valuable and even necessary dimension of it. And the possibilities of what today is often called "faith development" and what in the past was called "growth in grace" include this intellectual dimension. Studying theology can be personally enriching and even liberating. It provides opportunities for clearing up misunderstandings; for working through seeming conflicts between the world depicted in the Bible and contemporary scientific understanding of human nature and the natural world; for learning what, in fact, the church teaches, in contrast to widespread popular religious notions; and for discovering the insight and wisdom hidden deep within what otherwise seem to be dull formulas or empty clichés. There's more to the meaning and implications of the Christian faith than most people realize, and many find themselves enriched when they discover these unknown depths.

A Communal Reference Point

But as significant as such personal benefits are, the importance of studying theology is centrally connected to its *communal* character. Theologians are called upon to represent the *church*, not just their private opinions. And the work they carry on is meant to benefit the church as a whole, not just individual Christians. Significantly, twentieth-century theologian Paul Tillich opens the first volume of his magnum opus, *Systematic Theology*, with these words: "Theology, as a function of the Christian church, must serve the needs of the church. A theological system is supposed to satisfy two basic needs: the statement of the truth of the Christian message and the interpretation of this truth for every new generation."[1]

Tillich places theology right at the center of the Christian community, not at its margins. It is not something that is a luxury or an esoteric exercise restricted to a few interested individuals. It exists to enable the entire Christian community to work out its life and its mission. That's why at heart it is not a detached, self-contained, intellectual discipline. Rather, it exists to help the believing community understand

---

[1] Paul Tillich, *Systematic Theology*, vol. 1 (Chicago: University of Chicago Press, 1951), 3.

the gospel as clearly and faithfully as possible and see its unique implications for the present day.

This communal context distinguishes theology from other intellectual disciplines that can and do examine Christian faith and life. Sociology of religion, for example, can study how church life supports or criticizes American civic values or how local congregational life is shaped by factors of economic or educational class. Psychology of religion can investigate the ways faith can develop as people mature or can describe how neuroticism masquerades as piety. Philosophy of religion can analyze logical puzzles about concepts of God, including the conundrum: If God is omnipotent, can God create a rock too heavy for God to move? It also can take up deeply moving questions, such as, If God is omnipotent and loving, why is there so much random and unjust suffering in the world? History of religions can trace patterns shared by a variety of religions, including Christianity, such as the theme of the suffering savior figure or the use of the tree as a symbol. But theology is the scholarly discipline by which the church attempts to understand its own faith.

Therefore, Christian theology is not equivalent to the private opinions or even the majority opinions of church members. Its task is *prescriptive,* not descriptive. In other words, it is not concerned with identifying what the majority of Christians believe and do but rather seeks to prescribe what they *ought* to believe and do. Its aim is to speak *normatively* on behalf of the community's foundation in Jesus Christ.

Church members may have a variety of views about Jesus, for example, and may feel very differently about him. But theology, speaking for the church, tries to be clear about how the primitive Christian community viewed Jesus and what that should mean in the present contexts of culture and history. And in doing so, theology may very well find itself pitted against widespread popular opinions. In fact, one of its purposes is to present a normative interpretation of the gospel, as opposed to the folk religion and civil (that is, cultural) religion that can sometimes shape the belief and life of persons more than orthodox Christianity does.

As we have already noted in passing, this study is conducted so that the concrete aspects of the church's life can be given guidance. Centrally it means shaping the preaching and teaching work of the church. But it also seeks to hold up a faithful and relevant vision of the church's mission to the world, guide the ethics and worship and congregational life of Christians, and give direction to pastoral care.

The Need for a Theologically Aware Laity

One of the great challenges that the Christian community faces today is the fact that increasingly theology has been left to the ordained clergy, and far too often they have left it to the professional theologians who teach and write. Earlier we noted the pragmatic character of American culture. We are interested in doing, not thinking; we tend to assume theory is irrelevant. But the fact is that ideas *are* real. They change individuals and they can affect the world. We've noted how ideas created the American republic and established its system of legal rights. The *idea* that each person has equal value and dignity under the law not only is the basis for confronting and repudiating racism, it has shaped our judicial system. The same holds true for theological insights and affirmations. They can make a real difference for those who come to understand them and take them to heart. Let's look at just one example.

To affirm, as the scripture does, that the entire universe and all its component elements are the creation of God and that God views all of it as "lip-smackingly good," to use Robert Farrar Capon's words, affects how people look at the world. This theological affirmation of the value of embodied existence, of material reality, is reinforced by the Christian insistence that God's very life connected itself to the specific humanity of the human being Jesus. God became incarnate, which is to say God became "enfleshed," in him. To take the doctrines of creation and incarnation seriously means to value and respect the material world and our humanity, of which it is a part. As C. S. Lewis once remarked, "God loves matter; he invented it."

What's important to note is that from the church's origins, far too many Christians have refused to take this idea, this affirmation, to heart. They have misunderstood or ignored what the Hebraic and primitive Christian traditions teach and have believed ideas that even run contrary to this doctrine. In fact, the earliest distorted theology that the church had to fight, a movement called Gnosticism, thought precisely in these ways. Persons then and since and even now have had bad theology, and the results have been destructive. They have disparaged the material. They have said, in effect, "Heaven is my home." This world doesn't matter, since it is already perishing and ultimately will be destroyed by God. Consequently, when James Watt was Secretary of the Interior he admitted that, even though he was the official governmental watchdog for the environment, he did not have a deep concern about it. His religious views led him to believe that the world was going to end, and soon. Therefore, there was no reason to care about legislation, or enforcement of legislation, that sought to preserve and improve the natural environment for future generations.

This disregard for the integrity of the material world has been reinforced by a particular reading of the passage in Genesis (1:28) where God instructs human beings to "fill the earth and *subdue* it" and to "have *dominion*" over other animal life (emphasis added). Those are strong words, since the original Hebrew words mean something like "trample underfoot" and "rule over." Such language seems to give human beings permission, even outright encouragement, to reshape the world according to human desires. It seems to imply that there are no reasons to worry about other species of animals and plants, since they only exist to serve human needs. In fact, some historians believe it was this biblical mandate that encouraged the emergence of modern technology in European culture, which was influenced by Christianity.[2]

Careful and informed theology can show how these operating assumptions—and the concrete actions they encourage—are theologically unwarranted. We don't have the time to go into detail here, but let me make a few basic observations. Take, for example, the popular reading of Paul's

---

[2] A helpful examination of this issue by a variety of scholars can be found in the book edited by Eileen and David Spring, *Ecology, Religion and History* (New York: Harper & Row, 1974).

contrast between "life according to the spirit" and "life according to the flesh." (See Rom. 8:1–11 and Gal. 5:16–26 as examples.) This seems to endorse a view that material existence is inferior to a heavenly one. But when Paul contrasts "the spirit" and "the flesh," he is not deprecating the body and certainly not, like many believe, repudiating sex. He is not saying that our embodied life in the material world is of no importance. Instead, he is contrasting two ways of living in the world. One is rooted in the imperishable—that is, in God's own eternal existence ("the spirit"). The other assumes that things that perish ("the flesh") are worth giving one's life to. But the things of "the flesh" rot and decay like the ground-up flesh of animals, like uncooked hamburger sitting in the Mediterranean sun. Paul's concern is parallel to Jesus' injunction not to treasure things that can disintegrate or be taken away (Mt. 6:19–21; Lk. 12:33–34).

An additional theological observation is that disparaging our own embodied existence and the material world around us fails to take seriously the genuine humanity of Jesus. It does not understand the doctrine of the incarnation and the insistence of the early church that Christ was fully human. If Christians took seriously God's investment of God's own life in the genuine stuff of human life and history, their attitudes toward the environment and the choices and policies shaped by those attitudes might well be different from the ones that dominate our culture. There is a theological suspicion that those who call themselves Christians and who have no real concern for the planetary ecosystem also don't take Jesus' humanity very seriously. It's as if Jesus' humanity is assumed to be a kind of outer wrapper, a costume, that God wears. It is not an affirmation of the early Christian creed that the eternal Son of God "*became* man."[3] The same sort of confusion was found in the earliest centuries of Christian history, when persons known as Gnostics held to precisely this set of views, centering on a

---

[3]The Nicene Creed was originally formulated in 325 C.E. by a council of almost three hundred bishops who served as the church's theologians in that day. The larger statement about Christ is, "who for us, and for our salvation, came down from heaven; by the power of the Holy Spirit he became incarnate from the virgin Mary, and was made man."

disparagement of the material world and embodied existence. In fact, the earliest creeds were drawn up to reject these distorting assumptions. Even if it is not the prime cause for persons' disregard for the material world and aggrandizing attitudes toward the environment, not taking seriously biblical doctrine of creation and the orthodox Christian insistence on the genuine and full humanity of Jesus tends to reinforce such attitudes.

Or, to follow through on this a bit further, if one looks closely at the theology of the person who wrote the first chapter of Genesis, one notes a reference to human beings being created in God's "image." The implication of such an assertion is that human beings are created to reflect God in the way in which they deal with themselves, each other, and the world. In the ancient world, an image of the emperor was set up in marketplaces to indicate that, even though he was not physically present, he was *effectively* present. His authority and power to shape affairs was expressed through his image. In parallel fashion, the local governor whom the emperor sent to rule in his stead was, in effect, the living "image" of the emperor. Therefore, since human beings are created in God's image, the implication is that they are to exercise *God's* lordship, *God's* will, in regard to the world—not their own! To be the "image" of God means being God's representative. God's loving governance of the earth is now delegated to human beings. Furthermore, telling people to "subdue" the earth means one thing if they are people who have a primitive technology and who have access to limited amounts of power—wind for sails, running water to turn wheels, and the energy of certain animals and their own bodies. It means something far different in the modern context, when our technology and sources of power can make massive intrusions into the ecosystem.[4]

---

[4]For an examination of some implications of Genesis 1, see Lee Humphrey's essay "Pitfalls and Promises of Biblical Texts for a Theology of Nature," in *A New Ethic for a New Earth*, edited by Glenn C. Stone (New York: Friendship Press for the Faith-Man-Nature Group, 1971), 99–118. To investigate the concept of "image of God," see Douglas John Hall, *Imaging God: Dominion as Stewardship* (Grand Rapids: Eerdmans; New York: Friendship Press, for the Commission on Stewardship of the National Council of the Churches of Christ in the U.S.A., 1986).

My point here is a simple one. Ideas are real and have concrete effects. Poorly grounded ideas or ideas that misunderstand the intent of scripture or the church's understanding of God and the world have consequences that run counter to the will of God. They misrepresent authentic, informed Christian teaching. And, therefore, they enable persons who claim to be Christian to act in ways that deny what acknowledging the lordship of Christ means. What makes the difference? In part, it rests on doing careful and informed theology.

There is a growing concern that too many in the church ignore theology or believe it should rest in the hands of professionals. The shaping of church life in America by congregational committees and governing boards and by regional and national legislative bodies involves large numbers of laity. If the church is to be shaped by faithfulness to the gospel, it needs theologically informed laity who know how to think through issues carefully. Certainly this becomes obvious as churches struggle with volatile social issues such as abortion and homosexuality. But it also calls for lay leaders who know the clear outlines of Christian identity and mission, who have historical roots and spiritual integrity and are not confused with the general "religiousness" that characterizes much church life in America.[5]

The urgent need for theologically informed laity becomes even more apparent when one thinks about the need for Christians to provide moral and spiritual leadership for a world struggling with massive problems. One only has to think, for example, of the growing global disparity between rich and poor, the hunger for liberation and a respect for human rights on the part of marginalized people, or threats to the environment posed by an exploding consumer

---

[5] One can see this issue emerging, for example, as congregations are increasingly tempted to adopt "entertainment evangelism." The goal is to make visitors feel as comfortable as possible by minimizing expectations of active participation. But in the process, the recognition that worship focuses on *God*, not an "audience," can be lost. See Marva Dawn, *Reaching Out Without Dumbing Down: A Theology of Worship for the Turn-of-the-Century Culture* (Grand Rapids: Eerdmans, 1995). For a profile of popular American religion that claims to be Christian but lacks continuity with the roots of historic Christianity, see Harold Bloom, *The American Religion* (New York: Simon and Schuster, 1992).

economy. How can the Christian community provide any effective leadership if it does not have an important segment of its membership that is theologically aware? Theology helps to clarify what the claims of the gospel mean and what God wills for the world. By taking the theological task seriously, laypersons can begin to shape their discipleship by informing it. Theology provides the opportunity for them to gain perspective, *theoria*, in order to shape and direct Christian involvement in the world.

The Christian Rabbi

At the same time, this implies that theology is the specific responsibility of Christian clergy. They must be the ones to call laity to theological responsibility and serve as the primary resources for theological training in local congregations. It is precisely because theological literacy is the *responsibility* of ordained clergy and others serving alternative forms of professional ministry in the church that the church approves, trains, and sets them aside for leadership through ordination or commissioning. This expectation makes important demands on persons called to professional church work, not only in their preparatory studies but also in recommended programs of continuing education.

The egalitarian character of American society is uncomfortable when any group of people is set aside from others. But we need to recognize that from its earliest days the church has set aside such persons and in subsequent history has usually expected them to have special training in theology. Even though Jesus appealed most widely to persons who had little or no formal education, he himself was called "rabbi," that is to say, "teacher." And one of the most important leaders within the primitive Christian community, Paul, studied under one the great rabbis of his day, namely, Gamaliel of Jerusalem. In fact, Paul used his rabbinic training in the service of the gospel.

Respect for learning has been present in Christianity from its inception and reflects its Jewish roots and the beginnings of the rabbinical tradition that was emerging at the same time.

The Importance of Theology 57

This rabbinical tradition has had a development that parallels the Christian church and has created the Judaism that we know today. What we have to remember is that Jewish religion in Jesus' day also included other influences and concerns, which ranged from the sacrificial system of the temple in Jerusalem, to military resistance to Roman occupation, to semi-monastic community life.

But from the time of the Babylonian exile, which witnessed the destruction of the temple in Jerusalem and the dismantling of political life, Jews gathered together—especially in Babylon—to study the Torah (Law), sing psalms, and pray. This practice kept alive their religious faith and their national and cultural identity. Eventually this custom developed into the institutions of both the synagogue (a Greek term meaning "a bringing together") and the rabbinate. These institutions took root in Jewish communities both in Palestine and in the Diaspora, that is, the Jewish dispersion among the Gentiles. The rabbis were not priests. They did not act as intermediaries between God and Israel by offering up sacrifices. Instead they were scholars and interpreters of the written and oral Torah that shaped Jewish life. They were preachers and teachers who codified the biblical writings, standardized the synagogue liturgy, and provided the Jewish community with intellectual and spiritual leadership.

Although Christianity developed on its own path, because it grew out of the same strands of Jewish life, it developed patterns similar to those of rabbinic Judaism. Synagogue life and worship found close parallels in the Christian congregation and its liturgy, and reliance on rabbis echoed in Christians setting aside congregational leaders through the laying on of hands. These leaders are variously described in the New Testament as elders ("presbyters"), preachers ("prophets"), teachers, overseers ("bishops"), and shepherds ("pastors"). Like rabbis, they had a central responsibility in preserving and interpreting the oral—and later written—transmission of the tradition, giving spiritual guidance to the life of the congregation and preserving and safeguarding Christian identity.

In a short while, the spiritual leaders of the Christian community were expected to reflect a capacity for learning and for interpreting the texts of the scriptures that was similar to the rabbinical tradition. By the end of the second century, a Christian house of studies was established in Alexandria. It was the first of what soon became a number of such schools and had intellectual ties with the city's other centers of learning. Collectively, these schools in the city were the equivalent of a university. Clement, the second head of the Christian school, was a distinguished scholar who was an expert in Greek philosophy and used it in developing a Christian theology. His most outstanding pupil, Origen, was a brilliant thinker as well and a prodigious scholar who wrote a remarkable number and variety of theological books. These examples point to the emergence of a rich tradition of Christian scholarship and teaching that eventually created the great universities of medieval Europe, special orders such as the Dominicans, Augustinians, and Jesuits that had scholarship as a central concern, and vast numbers of theological writings.

The importance of the Christian development of rabbinical interest in formal study should not be overstated, however. From the beginning, Christians recognized the value of other forms of insight and leadership. The gospels depict Jesus rebuking the scribes, who were the scriptural scholars of his day, and thanking God for hiding the meaning of his teaching from the wise and intelligent and revealing them to infants (Mt. 11:25). And even Paul, for all his rabbinical education, draws attention to the fact that the word of the cross is foolishness to human wisdom (1 Cor. 1:18–25). Moreover, the earliest congregational leaders appear to have been singled out on the basis of charismatic appeal, not on the basis of being learned.

For all the stress on learning, throughout Christian history qualifications and outright suspicions of Christian theology and study have surfaced in the name of spiritual humility, mystical insight, direct spiritual experience, and the committed life. Francis of Assisi, for example, became a powerful spiritual influence among Christians without having any formal theological education or even being ordained.

Nevertheless, Christians have found it helpful to have theologically trained persons give leadership to congregations. This was especially true of the Protestant Reformation, which reshaped the ordained priesthood along rabbinical lines. By making the proclamation of the Word and the administration of the sacraments their fundamental responsibility, pastors were expected to have a university education in order to equip them adequately for preaching and teaching. This central stress on education of the clergy is reflected in fact that, for many centuries, Protestant pastors were often the most highly educated members of local communities.

The Resident Theologian

Much has changed over the years. The most highly educated persons in the community are hardly ever clergy. Moreover, clergy have increasing numbers of responsibilities placed on them besides the traditional rabbinical ones—parish administration, pastoral counseling and spiritual direction, evangelism and stewardship, specialized ministries to youth and the aging, community organization, and political advocacy of behalf of the poor and oppressed and marginalized. Few would dispute the need for study in preparing for these various forms of ministry. But such education is more like something akin to professional training than to traditional studies in theology. In the process, the expectation that the parish minister or priest should serve as the "resident theologian" of the congregation has waned.

But the need for these congregational leaders to be conversant with theology has not disappeared, even though it does not have the recognition by both clergy and laity that it once had. Note that among Protestants the preaching and teaching office is still regarded as primary, even if only in a formal way, and among Roman Catholics it has gained prominence since the second Vatican Council.

Unfortunately, even though expectations are high, there is widespread agreement among scholarly investigators and even rank and file congregational members that the quality of preaching has deteriorated significantly over the last generation. This may be due in part to the large number of demands being placed on parish clergy. But some suspect it is also due to a definite decline in interest in continuing theological study on the part of the ordained. Perhaps it is no accident that few today speak of the minister's or priest's *study*, but rather refer to his or her *office*.

Only solid study, however, can enable preachers and teachers of God's Word to be faithful to that calling. Simply rehashing biblical texts is not preaching any more than is resorting to telling charming stories. There are a number of theologians today who believe that the biblical meaning of the term *Word of God* refers primarily to an *event*. The Word is not fundamentally the Bible. Rather, it is God's self-communication that *happens* when human words become vehicles for God's outreach into the world. And the paradigmatic context for this "word-event" is preaching. Like the material elements of water, bread, and wine used in the sacraments, human words can become the concrete bearers of God's presence and impact. Although there are no guarantees that anything the preacher says becomes the "Word of God," the responsibility of preachers is to have their sermons serve "the living voice of the gospel," as Luther put it.

This means speaking with power and with meaning. The preacher needs far more than snappy or entertaining illustrations, polished oratorical skills, an impressive pulpit "presence," or a stained-glass voice. Relying on techniques such as these may entertain hearers, but it doesn't faithfully serve the preaching office. Only an informed and faithful perspective on the Christian biblical and churchly tradition and an equally informed and thoughtful perspective on what is going on in human experience can make God's Word present and effective. Only solid theological insight can make that Word come alive. That's because, as we noted Tillich pointing out, theology's task is to make clear the *truth* of the gospel and provide insightful interpretation of its meaning for today.

When people turn their attention to the pulpit, either implicitly or consciously, they are bringing with them their concrete lives and their wider world and are, in effect, asking,

"Is there any Word from the Lord?" They want to be able to see these ranges of human experience from *God's* perspective. And while sermons should hardly be lectures in theology, they need to be theologically *informed* if they are to serve this purpose. Only then can scripture and historical Christian memory illuminate the real issues occurring in the lived life, and only then can these issues make the wisdom and insight of scripture and the Christian tradition come alive with a living impact.

I vividly recall hearing Tillich, who is acknowledged to be one of the great theologians of this century, preach while I was a seminary student. From the standpoint of preaching techniques, Tillich did everything wrong. He read his manuscript, had no eye contact with his listeners, used no illustrations, and spoke in a somewhat monotone voice that had a thick German accent. Yet everyone listened intently, and I found myself craning forward from the edge of the pew. In part it was to catch his words, but mostly it was because I was transfixed. Decades later, I can still remember major themes of that sermon. Why? Because he had something to say! Tillich's preaching was great preaching not because he mastered flashy techniques but because he had *insight*. And he had insight because he did his theological homework.

Not many can be a Paul Tillich. But persons who step into a pulpit should have something to say. And they can only do that if they have insight into the Bible and the rich tradition of church teaching and into the concrete issues of human life. If persons with even modest gifts can be theologically responsible for the sake of their preaching, they will find an appreciative response from the pew. And, by God's grace, they may even eventually hear the words "Well done, my good and faithful servant."

In addition, the need for ordained persons who are theologically aware is also related to the need for more vigorous programs of adult education in the parish, which I referred to earlier. Large numbers of laypersons—for all their knowledge about the wider world and their specialized vocational training and even advanced education—have very rudimentary levels of theological understanding. And as I've already indicated, my experience in leading adult study groups in congregations with a variety of social and educational profiles has made me realize how hungry some people are for theologically solid study. Though their numbers may not be huge and may vary from one congregation to another, they're considerable enough to warrant intentional ministry. But in order to carry out this ministry, ministers and priests need to give conscious and extensive energy to theological study themselves.

All of this is not to say that pastors and priests are only Christian rabbis, resident theologians. On the contrary, modern ministry has many facets, and those serving that ministry need a variety of capabilities. But it is true that when they neglect theology, they soon begin to undermine the centrality of the ministry of Word and sacrament. Relying on the little perspective they gained in their seminary education, they eventually run out of steam or simply repeat themselves. They start preaching about their own personal enthusiasms or opinions rather than witnessing to the faith of the church. And when their ministries of preaching and teaching start to decline, they begin to have the specifically Christian dimensions of their office erode. Increasingly they are tempted to turn to a managerial model of being the executive of a small business or to a professional model of handing out specialized services of one sort or another to an appreciative clientele.

But even the nonrabbinical dimensions of ministry—parish administration, evangelism, counseling, and the like—suffer when they are no longer guided by the perspective on Christian identity and mission that theology provides. Without theological perspective, ordained persons become busy administrators concerned about statistical growth or chaplains serving the self-identified religious needs of individuals. They have increasingly less and less to do with the gospel. Consequently, even though the call to be the resident theologian, the Christian rabbi, is not the whole of ministry, it should be a constant reference point. And even though those seeking ordination needn't be preoccupied with theology or skilled at it, they should be knowledgeable and competent.

Summary

- Theology helps people integrate their faith and the wider world in which they live, particularly as life experience and education encourage them to raise probing questions and see life differently.

- The primary purpose of theology, however, is to serve the life of the Christian community by investigating and expressing the truth and meaning of the gospel. In doing so, theology does not represent the views of the majority, but instead seeks to be faithful to the gospel itself.

- In this regard, there is increasing recognition of the need for theologically informed laity, even while the evidence suggests widespread theological illiteracy.

- The church's expectation that ordained persons have the responsibility to be theologically informed goes back to the existence of the rabbinate, which provided intellectual and spiritual leadership for the Jewish community.

- The developing Christian tradition showed great respect for learning and for the theological training of ordained leaders. This was balanced by the recognition that life in Christ is not equivalent to scholarship.

- Historical and cultural shifts have eroded the expectation that ordained leaders are to be "resident theologians" in the congregation. But the need still remains to the extent that the importance of preaching and teaching is still recognized.

- Only theological insight can make preaching have a vitality and power that rests on the impact of God's Spirit and not on slick techniques or psychological manipulation.

- Without a commitment to maintain theological insight, the rabbinical ministry degenerates and ordained persons are reduced to being business executives or private chaplains.

For Further Reading and Reflection

The impact of providing laypersons with theological training often has surprising results that have been picked up by sociological analysis.

The public impression about the private college at which I taught was that it has a religiously conservative faculty and student body because of its very close connections to the church. This is a widely held assumption that many people have of such schools. However, the sociology department of the college and of two larger state universities located in the same metropolitan area conducted research to check this out. The results confirmed the direct opposite of this popular assumption. Overall, religious views of students and faculty at the church-related college were much more sophisticated, informed, and qualified than those of students and faculty at the state schools. There, religion, and Christianity in particular, was understood much more simplistically. This resulted not only in a naïve enthusiasm for religion but also an equally naïve rejection of it.

The data suggested that the presence on campus of faculty serving in the religion department and a significant number of required courses in religion were the primary reasons for this disparity. It seems that theology *does* make a difference. How do you respond to this possibility?

5

The Goals of Theology

To this point we have already noted some broad descriptions of the nature and purposes of theology. Saint Anselm has spoken of "faith seeking understanding," that is, thinking about believing by using thinking that already believes. Paul Tillich has described theology as a communal function that the church carries out in order to understand the truth of the gospel and discover its contemporary relevance.

We have also observed that theology aims at providing perspective on the church's faith and life, guiding its mission to the world and its own inner preaching and teaching life. In this connection we've identified theology as an intellectual discipline that works with ideas and that crafts theories. For this reason, theology is as much connected to the academy as it is to the church. In other words, it is as capable of being studied and taught in academic settings as in congregational ones. And as disciplined reflection, theology takes into account wide ranges of human discovery and insight as it attempts to understand both the business of being Christian and the business of being human and how they intersect.

But now it is appropriate to look at the nature and purposes of theology in greater detail.

Theology as a Rational Discipline

One of the most important questions that is debated in theological circles is how the faith of the church is to be related to human reason. You will find this is one of the basic topics of theological prolegomena. Not surprisingly, theology's concerns with this relation, and with the parallel relation between the authority of revelation and scripture on the one hand and the authority of rational analysis on the other, have brought it into close contact with many forms of human learning. But it has had special connections to philosophy, since philosophy is centrally concerned with rationality itself.

Clement of Alexandria, whom we've already discussed, was one of the first Christian intellectuals to appreciate philosophy and use it in his theological work. He did so because he believed that in the final analysis Christ himself is the source of all valid philosophical reflection and insight. He writes:

> God is responsible for all good things: of some, like the blessings of the Old and New Covenants, directly; of others, like the riches of philosophy, indirectly. Perhaps philosophy too was a direct gift of God to the Greeks before the Lord extended his appeal to [them]. For philosophy was to the Greek world what the Law was to the Hebrews, a tutor escorting them to Christ. So philosophy is a preparatory process; it opens the road for the person whom Christ brings to his final goal.[1]

In using philosophy as an aid, Clement was a forerunner of a major tradition known today as *philosophical theology*, which, as the name indicates, appreciates such close connections.[2] Philosophical theology's conscious goal is a synthesis of philosophical arguments and traditional church teaching. A classic example is found in Thomas Aquinas' treatment of

---

[1] *Stromateis*, I:5 (trans. John Ferguson), in Thomas P. Halton, et al., eds., *Fathers of the Church* (Washington, D.C.: Catholic University of America Press, 1991).

[2] Philosophical theology will be explored further in chapter 6.

the doctrine of God. He points to what he believes are rational proofs for the existence of God. One need not be a Christian to believe in God; one only has to think carefully about our experience of the world. But philosophical argument is insufficient in Thomas' view. All philosophical analysis can do is to tell us *that* God is, but it cannot tell us *what* God is. To understand the nature and will of God we are dependent on God's self-disclosure, God's revelation. We must come to meet God incarnate in Jesus Christ.[3]

Philosophical theology has been criticized both by philosophers and by theologians. From the philosophical side, specifically in the last few centuries, serious questions have been raised about the capacity of human consciousness to know very much, if anything, outside itself. Immanuel Kant argued that we cannot know things as they are in and of themselves, but only as they impact us through our senses and are given recognition and form by the pattern of our minds. Building on this, many now believe that any speculations about the ultimate nature of reality—and certainly about God—are beyond us. Consequently, philosophy can't provide theology with any raw materials.[4]

From the theological side, there has always been a suspicion that philosophy tends to reduce Christian faith to its own categories and misses the unique temperament and insight of faith. So Tertullian, an equally celebrated theologian and contemporary of Clement, could jibe, "What does Jerusalem have to do with Athens?!" Believing philosophical theology to be bloodless and incapable of communicating the living faith witnessed to in the Bible, Luther dismissed it as the invention of "Sophists." And in our own day there has been widespread assumption that theology needs to build on its own unique foundations.[5] At the same time, there is still a third group of theologians, who hold that while

---

[3]See *On the Truth of the Catholic Faith [Summa Contra Gentiles]: Book One—God*, trans. Anton C. Pegis (Garden City, N.Y.: Doubleday, 1955), chap. 3.

[4]Actually Kant tried to do this, but in connection with what he called "practical reason," that is, the moral capacities of human consciousness.

[5]This is the movement known as "neo-orthodoxy," which will be reviewed in chapter 6.

theology and philosophy are distinct from each other, they can be related to each other in valid and creative ways.

The question of the potential relations between theology and philosophy has very important implications for how theologians construct their theology. But whatever they conclude, it certainly is the case that most would want to carry out theology with the same intellectual care and rigor as any other responsible study. And even if theologians don't necessary "buy into" particular philosophical theories, in one way or other they do have to come to grips with two basic philosophical issues.

Philosophy literally means "love of wisdom" in Greek. And it is well named, since philosophers are persons who love to know. They love trying to get at the basic principles underlying human conduct, thought, and the existence of the universe. In some wonderful way they haven't lost the curiosity of young children who refuse to take anything for granted. They're always making a nuisance of themselves by asking "Why?" "How?" "Can we be certain?" "Why should we believe that?" "Why are things the way they are, and what are they ultimately?"

This involves philosophers in *the* most basic questions that can be asked. One collection of questions revolves around our capacity to know all sorts of things. Each time we make an assertion, we are assuming we know something to be true. But what is the nature of such knowledge? And how can we test its validity? And do we know things in the same way? The technical term for this major concern of philosophy is *epistemology*. It is derived from the Greek word for knowledge.

In the course of a single day I could make a number of assertions about what I know to be the truth. "Two plus two is four." "The earth is round." "All in all, Truman was a good president." "Ice cream tastes better than raw lemons." "I love my spouse." In each case I am claiming to speak the truth. But closer examination shows that the *ways* in which I know these things to be so differ from each other. And if the truthfulness of my assertions were challenged, I would have to defend them differently.

So, for example, (assuming a base of ten) two and two are always four, since the very definition of "four" includes two "twos." Validity rests not on sense experience but on logic, and the logical patterning of all mathematics enables us to work on complicated mathematical cases. But we need the data of sense experience—by way of observations extended by the use of complicated machines—in order to theorize about the shape of the earth. And, of course, changing data or more coherent theories have caused us to refine our notions. So, we learned that the earth was round, not flat, and now today we know that it is slightly pear-shaped, not totally round. And when it comes to judgments about Truman, we need some agreement about what "good" means, and we have to evaluate his decision to drop atomic bombs on Japan. Validating a statement about love is even more complicated. It means we must not only know certain facts about the relationship and see how it coheres with certain values, but in the final analysis it calls on us to trust the person who makes the assertion.

The point is, we do not know everything in the same way. Certain forms of knowing—and, therefore, certain ways of arguing for the truthfulness of our knowledge—are more appropriate in some cases than in others. How then does this apply to religious convictions and statements of faith? Is the truth about God and Christ a matter of logical definition, or theorizing on the basis of sense observation, or value judgment, or what?

Even if theologians don't want to depend on particular philosophical systems, they have to deal with epistemological questions. They have to explain what sort of truth is implied in religious statements. They need to make clear how assertions about knowing God through "revelation" can be tested for their validity. They have to be able to explain how religious truth is distinguishable from superstition or nonsense. They need to be clear about what *kind of* knowledge is entailed in Christian faith.

Interestingly, in recent years the more traditional ways of approaching epistemological questions have been challenged by the discipline known as *sociology of knowledge*. This is the recognition that the ways in which we think about basic issues are limited by the particular cultures in which we live and are prejudiced by our own social, political, and economic interests. This means that we have to be aware of how these unconscious forces can prejudice claims about the truth. Inevitably we tend to favor claims to the truth that serve our self-interest. Being aware of this and factoring it into our interpretation of viewpoints is appropriately called a "hermeneutic of *suspicion*."

For example, wealthy persons in a capitalist country are usually the strongest advocates of the "obvious" truth of the supreme importance of the individual. But that shouldn't be surprising. This value helps them believe that their own initiative and merit has made them wealthy. It also gives them a good conscience when they have to face the issue of poverty, since it can be explained as primarily the fault of the poor themselves. And it provides the grounds for insisting that the government should not interfere in economic matters. A perfect fit. The implication is that championing individualism is not as obviously and unqualifiedly "good" as many sincerely believe it is. Their conviction of this being an unqualified "truth" is shaped by their unrecognized self-interest.

The recognition of the sociological basis for many of our truth claims has complicated the picture, but it makes facing epistemological issues even more important than ever.

Two other subdisciplines in philosophy are ethics and logic. They have relevance for what we might call the *shape* of theology. But theology's *content* is affected by epistemology and a fourth major philosophical concern. When we assert that something is true, we do not simply mean we *know* something about it; we also are claiming to know something about the way things *are*. This implies the need to be clear about what we assume to be the nature of reality. Philosophical reflection about this subject has traditionally been called *metaphysics*. The name is a historical accident, since Aristotle's major analysis of ultimate reality was listed *after* (*meta* in Greek) his book called the *Physics*, which treated the structure of nature (*physis* in Greek).

I've already referred to the epistemological "humility" that has shaped philosophy since Kant. For this reason, metaphysics has not found widespread modern support. But in this century a more modest form called *ontology* has emerged. Ontology does not pretend to describe the nature of ultimate reality and how everything from God to poetry to sexual love to subatomic particles fit together. Instead, it tries to simply describe outlines of the universally shared experience—the psychological awareness—of *being human* in the world. This limited scope accounts for the name, which comes from the Greek word *ontos*, meaning "being." Since ontology tries to trace the outlines of human *existence*, it is often known as *existential ontology*.

In Christian history, some theology has been deeply tied to metaphysics. Aquinas, the traditional Roman Catholic theology that has made his work normative, Lutheran and Calvinist scholastics of the seventeenth century, and their traditionalist counterparts in the twentieth century have been deeply indebted to Aristotle. Many nineteenth-century theologians looked to Hegel and others in the philosophical school called *idealism* (distinguished from our usual use of the term). In our own century, some known as *process theologians* have relied on a metaphysical system created by mathematician Alfred North Whitehead that reflects what he saw as implications of modern physics.[6] And still others have depended on the existential ontology just referred to.

But even if contemporary interpreters of the Christian faith are not indebted to particular systems of metaphysics or ontology, they inevitably have to put their metaphysical cards on the table. They need to explain, if they do nothing else, in what way God is real and how God is related to the rest of reality. No one avoids metaphysical assumptions any more than epistemological ones. If Christians are going to speak about their faith responsibly, then they have to face these issues.

Interestingly, just as there have been contemporary challenges to the traditional ways epistemological issues have been developed, so there are equivalents in regard to

---

[6]We will look at this briefly in the next chapter.

metaphysics. The argument is being made that we need to focus on what some are calling *metachronics*, in distinction from metaphysics. The most significant feature of the human experience of reality is the pervading sense of *time* (*chronos* in Greek). This is theologically relevant, since there is wide consensus that the Hebrew and Christian scriptures depict a God who is deeply involved and essentially known in history. Traditional metaphysics, in contrast, is more interested in what is permanently the case. Consequently, it can have a relatively static view of reality in contrast to the more dynamic outlooks of scripture and modern science. Perhaps metachronics can provide categories for understanding what is "real" in a way that can be helpful for Christian understanding of the basic assumptions of the Bible.

To summarize, in its centuries of development, theology has often had a close relationship with philosophy. Coming to know something about the historical development of each and their interaction with each other will be valuable in your study of theology. Again, be patient and use some judgment here. You should not assume that you need to know it all or know it in detail. But sometimes philosophical background can prove helpful, and your effort in thinking about philosophical questions can be worth the effort. That's because your unconscious epistemological and metaphysical assumptions determine much, from how you read the Bible to what you think about traditional notions such as "eternal," "creation," or "divine providence."

General Purposes

Most of the references that have been made to "theology" have not distinguished between the broad and more specialized uses of the term. We ought to do that now.

Broadly speaking, "theology" refers to all forms of disciplined study that are carried on by the church, are used to train church leaders—particularly those who are ordained—and that guide church witness and practice. Therefore, large segments of seminary education are included under the heading *practical theology*, that is, disciplined study of various aspects of the practice of ministry and mission. The term is connected to the Greek word *praxis*, meaning "activity" or "plan of action." Included are studies of administration, preaching, education, counseling, interpersonal skills, leading small groups, and the like.

If you review the list again, you will see that each of these concerns can be approached from what we could call "secular" standpoints. Training in public speaking can inform preaching. Educational psychology can help the church's teaching ministry. Knowing something about management skills and problem solving can be a great asset in administering the life of a congregation. And so on. And practical theology does use such insight. But what makes it "theology" is its concern to also see what implications life in Christ and the unique mission of the church apply to these areas. For example, even though the developing skills in public speaking and composition can aid preaching, theology can put it in special perspective. As we've noted, some theologians link preaching to a recognition of the "Word of God" as an event, as something that happens to people. Perhaps you can begin to see how this theological understanding can affect how preachers approach their task as much as developing skills in rhetoric can.

A special focus under the wider heading of practical theology is *pastoral theology*. This is study of the nature of the pastoral office. It goes far beyond listing duties and providing advice about how best to fulfill them. It takes up the question of pastoral identity and of what is called pastoral or priestly *formation*. In other words, it tries to understand how best to shape persons spiritually so they become Christ's shepherds not simply in what they do, but in what they are, in how they live out their calling.

One of the most indispensable expressions of theology is the careful scholarship that is carried on by those who take up the task of helping the church understand its own roots as carefully and as honestly as it can. These theologians are historians in the widest sense of the term. History is far more than what its widespread presentation in public suggests, namely, the boring account of "one damn thing after another," as someone put it. Instead, history entails discerning the significance and interconnectedness of events. It calls attention to what we *make* of events, *how* we see them.

The collapse of the Soviet Union, for example, can be interpreted as the result of the West's military buildup bankrupting the parallel Soviet response. But it also can be interpreted as being due to purely internal factors. This question of interpretation also holds true for the history of the churches, such as their interactions with the rise of Renaissance humanism. Historians trace the significance, the legacy, the ongoing relevance of the past. And what is *made* of this past has a shaping influence on how the contemporary Christian community sees itself.

Church historians investigate and explain what we could call *institutional history*, that is, the history of the church as it is set in the wider flow of social events. They trace the transformations that have shaped the Christian community over time as it has evolved in differing cultures and eras. They provide interpretation of historical developments ranging from the rise of monasticism to the interplay that took place between the emerging power of the middle class and the Reformation.

But church historians also are concerned with what is known as *the history of Christian thought*. This historical study examines how the doctrinal traditions of the churches have developed and what forces account for them. It also traces the history of theology itself and how the self-interpretation of the Christian faith has responded to its contemporary environments. It interprets, for example, how ways of interpreting Jesus have reflected prevailing social values or how American political philosophy has had congenial connections to particular forms of Protestantism. This specialized study is closely associated with a little-known but intriguing discipline called *the history of ideas*. We needn't elaborate on its importance here but need only think back to what has already been said about the power of emerging ideas.

Since the most important aspect of Christian history is its origins, particularly the person and ministry of Jesus and his own roots in Israel, the most influential historical study that is carried out is done by biblical scholars. Like all historians, they are interested in what they can learn from archeological finds, but they work primarily with texts. In doing so they use the methods of historical scholarship that are employed by nonbiblical historians in reading documents from the past. In fact, biblical scholars developed many of these methods in the first place. It's quite astounding to realize that modern Christian scholars were the very first representatives of a religious community to subject its sacred writings to intense critical analysis.

These studies play an important role in *hermeneutics*. This widely used term, which comes from the Greek verb meaning "explain" or "interpret," refers to the development of an informed and rationally defensible method of biblical interpretation. Modern hermeneutics depends greatly on what is known as *historical criticism*. Using an approach that at times parallels sophisticated detective work, scholars examine biblical texts in order to make educated guesses about the date, setting, and purpose of the text, the probable audience for which it was intended, and what can be said about the author or authors. Such investigations even theorize about earlier forms of the writings that predate the texts we have, or earlier written or oral sources that the author might have used.

Such analysis can aid the goal of interpreting these written materials on their own terms by placing them in specific contexts, particularly ones that differ markedly from our own. For example, because they lived in a prescientific world, ancient people did not distinguish the "natural" and the "supernatural" as we do. Therefore, they did not understand miracles as divine suspension of the laws of nature. They certainly saw that nature had regularities, but they had no sense of nature being a self-enclosed, self-explaining system. When it rained, it did so because God made it happen, just as God could make the sun stand still or turn water into wine. But the latter instances would be seen as powerful and special signs of God's presence and will at work. Therefore, we should not assume that the effect that biblical references to miracles had on their original readers are the same as their effect on us today.

This should cause us to think twice about the ways in which we usually respond to references to Jesus performing miracles. For us, these appear to be clear evidence that Jesus is the special agent of God, if not the divine Son of God himself. But if we place these accounts in their historical setting, it isn't obvious that Jesus would be understood as defying the laws of nature, since no one then had any such notion. Rather, the conclusion would be either that he was a person with great authority and power or that God was working through him. The development of modern science is responsible for interpretations that see these accounts in terms of "the supernatural."

Nor should we assume that Jesus is the only worker of miracles as far as the original readers of the text were concerned. On the contrary, there is historical evidence that large numbers of such claims were made. This is even mentioned in the New Testament itself with regard not only to Peter, Paul, and Barnabas but even to persons unrelated to Jesus (Mt. 12:27; Lk. 11:19). And there still survive carved testimonials that were set up by pilgrims who found healing at the shrine of Epidauros in Greece dedicated to the demi-god Aesclepius. All sorts of people, such as kings, were assumed to be capable of dispensing what we call "miraculous" healing. In fact, the practice of having kings lay their hands on sick people persisted even into the eighteenth century. This shows how careful historical investigation can shape our interpretation of scripture.

In addition, historical criticism is supplemented by what is called *literary criticism.* Often these distinguishable disciplines flow into one another in the work of biblical scholarship. The distinctive focus of literary criticism, however, is an examination of texts that takes up issues beyond those of historical and cultural background. There is interest, for example, in the kind of writing that a particular text represents. We read different kinds of texts in differing ways. For example, we not only have to distinguish between fiction and nonfiction, we even make interpretative distinctions between forms of literature that are related to each other. We read novels differently than fairy tales and editorials differently than news stories. We would even read entries in a private diary differently than we would the letters of the same person.

Staying with biblical accounts of miracles, we can see how literary analysis can be instructive. Scholars have discovered parallel stories in nonbiblical texts coming from a variety of sources. In certain instances they have even discovered a set pattern in nonbiblical sources for telling healing stories that is mirrored in the accounts about Jesus. This does not warrant saying that Jesus never had a healing impact on sick persons. But it does mean that the accounts that we have were creatively shaped by the early church's interest in communicating a "portrait" of Jesus in his spiritual significance. To do this the church used all the resources at its disposal, including the literary form of healing stories found in pagan literature.

Literary analysis also has noted that texts tend to develop a life of their own that goes far beyond the conscious intention of their authors. A highly acclaimed television series on the American Civil War used excerpts from private letters and diaries. Certainly those who wrote these texts never assumed their writings would be known to so many people and certainly never dreamed that they would be used this way. But what they wrote surpasses their original and conscious intentions. Their writings enable readers more than a century later to understand not simply their personal stories but the wider events of which they were a part. The approach to understanding biblical texts this way is known as *narrative criticism*. It recognizes how biblical writings develop an independence from their authors and their original readers and create a series of responsive audiences differing not only from the original one but even from each other.

But the issue of biblical interpretation forces us to go beyond the work of historical and literary scholarship. In the first chapter, we saw that we had to be clear about our own presuppositions in approaching scripture. Why do we believe they are authoritative—or aren't? What sort of authority do they have and how is it recognized? How can the claims of scripture be related to other claims, such as coherence with scientific understandings of human nature and the universe?

This is the point at which Christians need to wrestle with epistemological and metaphysical assumptions and implications. They need to be clear about how we interpret, prioritize, and integrate scripture. They need to be aware of how we integrate its claims and concerns with those that arise in the wider arena of human knowledge, and they need to substantiate our way of doing this. In other words, they need to take up a whole range of questions that have us identify and integrate the entire spectrum of Christian beliefs and see how they are rationally defensible and coherent. These are the concerns of *systematic theology*.

Systematic Theology

Systematic theology has its roots in the Christian community's interest in systematizing its teaching (or "doctrine," as it is often called because of the Latin word for teaching, *doctrina*). Such systematizing helped the church catechize persons and prepare them for baptism and entrance into the community by identifying and integrating the various assertions the church made about a number of topics and issues. Systematizing also helped church theologians identify and argue for consistencies in such teaching. For example, as we have already noted, one cannot consistently assert that Jesus was truly human, the very incarnation ("en-flesh-ment") of God, and then believe that the human body is basically evil or, to push the implications further (as we have already noted), that concern for the environment has nothing to do with Christian identity.

In traditional Protestant circles, systematic theology—or *dogmatics*, as it was called—amounted to organizing and integrating church teaching through systematizing what scholars believed the Bible taught. Because they emerged in so many differing contexts and are expressed in so many different literary forms, biblical views do not have any self-evident coherence and certainly no integrated or consistent way of speaking. It was an early aim of theology to provide this integration and consistency.

Over a period of time, the systematic and coherent presentation of Christian doctrine took on the outline found in the great creeds of the church. These are the Nicene Creed, which emerged from the first ecumenical council in 325 C.E. and established certain elements of orthodox ("catholic") teaching about Christ, and the Apostles' Creed, which traces its roots back to the baptismal confession of faith used by Christians in Rome at the end of the third century. Out of the pattern of these creeds emerged the custom of exploring specific topics, or *loci* (meaning "locations" in Latin), grouped under headings that were connected with the three "articles" of the creeds, which refer to God the Father, God the Son, and God the Holy Spirit.

Under the first article, theology touched on such loci as the nature of God, the Trinity, creation, and providence. The major preoccupations of the second article are the "person" and "work" of Christ. The former explores Christ's relation to both God and to humanity, while the latter takes up with the meaning and means of salvation. But in order to understand these adequately, either under the first or second article, attention is given to the Christian teaching about human nature and its perversion in sin. Consequently, reference to evil is also made. The third article touches on the meaning and purpose of the church, sacraments, worship and prayer, the end of history, and life beyond death.

Eventually this systematic treatment of church teaching became known as *dogmatics*. Unfortunately, the term *dogmatic* has a highly pejorative ring to it in our own day. It seems to refer to asserting something to be true in an authoritarian fashion without referring to any supporting evidence. But theological usage refers to a systematic way of thinking through and presenting church teaching. The term itself, like so many others, emerged in church history and comes from the Greek word for teaching, *dogma*, and therefore is parallel to the Latin term *doctrina*.

In this century, some of the most influential work in systematic theology has been that of Swiss Protestant theologian Karl Barth. He purposely titled his multi-volume work *Church Dogmatics* because his self-conscious aim was a theology that spoke for the church to the church without any attempt to argue the case of Christian faith to those outside the church. In other words, even though he used the insights of modern scholarship and asked critical questions, Barth insisted that the fundamental concern of theology is to faithfully explore the truth given in God's revelation. Theology should not be concerned with communication outside the circle of faith. For this reason, he avoided the term *systematic theology* and preferred speaking about *dogmatics*.[7]

The elements of systematic theology that Barth wanted to avoid are traditionally known as *natural theology* and *apologetics*. Natural theology is often misunderstood as referring to what can be known about God by an examination of nature. While natural theology does in fact concern itself with such possibilities, it has a wider scope. It refers to what can be known about God by the natural capacities of human reflection, not simply what conclusions can be drawn from examining the natural world. It identifies the implicit knowledge of God reflected in philosophy and in the less sophisticated yet widespread religiousness that seems to be a natural part of human awareness and custom.

The breakdown of older alliances between philosophy and theology has been supplemented by the rise of scholarly skepticism about the nature of human religiousness. There are reasons to suspect that what was once called *natural religion* refers only to factors within the human psyche and human social relationships. The net effect has been to discredit earlier appeals to natural theology. This is what made Barth restrict himself to dogmatics. But a more qualified equivalent of natural theology has been at work in twentieth-century theology. Roman Catholic discussions have called this *fundamental theology*. This includes an analysis of how human experience, even though it does not reflect knowledge of God, continually points beyond itself. It is "self-transcending." To be human is to constantly live with an implicit reference to something ultimate that gives human activity, morality, and hope their basis.

As you can see, fundamental theology enables church theologians to make use of wide reaches of human thought and activity as raw material in speaking of how God and life are related. This is not to say that human expressions of

---

[7]See the discussion of "neo-orthodoxy" in chapter 6.

self-transcendence are of the same character or importance for Christians as coming to know God in Jesus Christ. But systematic theologians attempt to show how the two can be connected. One of the effects of making such connections is to help Christians integrate their faith with the wider reaches of human experience. Another is to present a defense of the rational integrity and consistency of Christian faith. This hardly will convert critics of the church. But it may help persons who do not recognize the reasonableness of Christian teaching and are thereby tempted to abandon their faith.

This interest in addressing criticisms and questions that come from outside the circle of faith is known as *apologetics*. Broadly speaking, we can say that just as dogmatics is the theological work of the church as it faces inward to its own life and its own foundation in Jesus Christ, so apologetics is its theological work as it faces outward to the wider world. It takes up issues and questions by looking for affirmations or standards of truth that are shared by Christians and non-Christians. Having established common ground, apologetics then constructs rationally supported arguments for Christian faith. Unfortunately, just as the term *dogmatics* has confusing connotations for modern English usage, so does the term *apologetics*. It sounds as if theologians are making excuses for Christianity and asking for forbearance. But like so many other terms we've discussed, apologetics comes from the Greek and at root means "speaking in defense" (*apo*, "from," and *logos*, "word"). In other words, one speaks out of one's convictions to those raising questions about them.

Apologetics has had strong support in the history of theology, reaching as far back as the account of Paul's speech to the Athenians found in Acts (17:22–31) and the *Apology of Aristides*, dating from the earliest part of the second century. Some of the earliest Christian theologians are called *apologists*, since their work consists primarily in responding to pagan or Jewish critics of Christianity by defending its truthfulness or integrity. Other apologists, like Clement of Alexandria, whom we have already discussed, try to build bridges between the best in secular culture and the faith and life of the church—particularly by using philosophy to demonstrate the faith's reasonableness.

Barth's rejection of apologetics rested on his belief that Christianity had sold its soul to middle-class European culture, that it had soft-pedaled the gospel's more abrasive implications. Others, such as Tillich, affirmed the value of apologetics. Significantly, he titled his major work *Systematic Theology*. While Tillich was critical of secular culture and argued for the uniqueness of the gospel, he insisted on the need for an "'answering theology'...[which] must answer the questions implied in the general human and the special historical situation."[8] Tillich's modified apologetics has parallels in the work of twentieth-century Roman Catholic theologians, who have moved from traditional appeals to natural theology to careful elaborations of what is called *fundamental theology*[9] and use the existential ontology mentioned above. As you can guess, this remains a major issue for theology.

Perhaps the most important feature of systematic theology has been its attempt to be as comprehensive as possible. It aimed at being *the* integrating discipline for the study of theology in all its many configurations. It not only tried to coordinate the variety of biblical and historical materials, but sought to relate these to philosophical understanding and all relevant analysis of human experience. This goal has assumed that educated persons who are highly disciplined and informed are capable of mastering the entire range of human knowledge. Systematic theologians were thought to be capable of doing this on behalf of the church and make clear the important relationships between these wide ranges of human knowledge and Christian doctrine. The resulting "system" they created went far beyond a systematizing of biblical materials or Christian teachings. It was a prodigious integration of the broad reaches of human knowledge and Christian self-understanding.

---

[8]Paul Tillich, *Systematic Theology*, vol. 1 (Chicago: University of Chicago Press, 1951), 31. Theology has moved on from the work of Barth and Tillich, but the issues they raised remain.

[9]See the entry under this name in *A Concise Dictionary of Theology*, edited by Gerald O'Collins and Edward G. Farrugia (New York/Mahwah, N.J.: Paulist Press, 1991).

This has proved an increasingly impossible goal. Human knowledge is expanding at an incredible rate with the rise of modern methods of scholarship. What is more, the various disciplines have developed their own particular methods that often have very little to do with each other. For example, not only do science and literature proceed differently, but so do their subdisciplines like quantum mechanics and molecular biology or drama and poetry. Today it is impossible to have a comprehensive integration of the many forms of human knowledge and even less a Christian version of one.

At the same time, the integrating goals of theology have not been abandoned. Systematic theologians still seek to make connections between biblical and church teaching and secular knowledge. But because no comprehensive system is possible and because theologians are never finished with the task of integration, some American theologians in the latter part of this century have suggested that the term *constructive theology* is the most appropriate one. Christian reflection cannot even dream of creating a comprehensive system. But it can fruitfully pursue the more modest task of building lines of significant connection in limited contexts and with regard to a specific range of issues.

As a result, some argue that today it is more important to help persons learn how to build theology than to encourage them to master a particular system. This becomes especially noticeable when theology is pursued in concrete contexts for ministry rather than in the academy. Certainly, people who live in a West Virginia coal mining town share some basic human concerns and experiences with affluent and highly educated upwardly mobile suburbanites outside San Francisco. But it's immediately obvious that the way "resident theologians" discern the meaning and implications of the gospel should differ in these different settings. Theology "in general" is not enough. It must also be constructed locally.

This same point is made by Latin American, African, and Asian Christians. Up to this point, theology has overwhelmingly had European roots. It has developed in dialogue with the great forces that have shaped this particular culture and its transplants in the Americas and elsewhere: the classical and medieval heritage, democracy, capitalism, colonialism, modern science and technology, and secularism. But in other cultural contexts, Christians must construct an indigenous theology that speaks to the particular issues and traditions that shape these non-European situations.

Consequently, some Latin American theologians have focused on the pressing issue of economic disparity that afflicts that region. They have used Marxian analysis (that is, specific political and social analysis) to understand what is going on. Within this particular context, they are constructing what is appropriately named *liberation theology*. Others also see the value of social analysis for constructing theologies to guide Christian witness and ministry in South Africa, poverty-stricken Asia, or even the hills of West Virginia or Marin County, California.

Numbers of non-European Christians are calling for an indigenous theology that builds apologetic bridges to local cultural traditions. Rather than linking up with Western philosophy or analyses of Western society, indigenous theologies are being constructed that intersect with traditional African religion, the ancient philosophical traditions of India and China and Japan, and the spirituality of Native American people. What is more, theologians in Europe and North America believe that their own churches can be enriched by the insight that emerges from these differing cultural contexts. Non-Europeans have wisdom that can benefit Christians everywhere. As a result, never before in Christian history has there been such theological pluralism. It is essential for students of theology to become acquainted with these expressions of theology as they seek to articulate the meaning of Christian faith and provide guidance for the church's ministry and mission.

Having noted the different terms that are used to speak of theology in the narrower sense of the term, and noting as well the special connotations these terms have, it is instructive to see which are used by particular theologians. If authors have "Christian Doctrine" or "Dogmatics" in their titles, you can expect the character of their work to differ significantly from those who refer to "Systematic" or

The Goals of Theology 85

"Constructive" theology. But whether theologians agree with the assumptions of constructive theology or not, they are all involved in a constructive process. They want to build a perspective on the faith and life of the church by using certain building materials and following a specific plan or method.

Summary

- Broadly speaking, *theology* refers to the disciplined academic study that is carried out by the Christian community for the sake of guiding its witness and practice.

- A subdiscipline known as *practical theology* draws on the insights of secular analysis to shape elements of the church's ministry and mission, but also asks what unique insights life in Christ provides. *Pastoral theology* does the same for shaping the calling of the ordained.

- Because it is concerned with the significance and interconnectedness of events, *historical theology* provides interpretation of both the church's institutional history and the history of Christian theology itself. Its results show the current relevance of church tradition.

- The most influential historical study that is carried on is that of biblical studies, which, using the methods of historical and literary analysis, look at particular segments of the Bible and contribute to the creation of a *hermeneutic*, that is, a carefully crafted theory of interpretation.

- *Dogmatics* is the term given to the systematic organization and integration of biblical and other church teaching organized around certain topics and usually presented in a pattern set by the creeds. *Apologetics* faces outward and relates church teaching to the wider secular and academic arena, often presenting a defense of Christian faith against its critics.

- The term *systematic theology* reflects not only the attempt to systematize Christian teaching, but also the attempt to do so in a comprehensive system that embraces the totality of human knowledge. Recognizing this as an impossible goal at present, *constructive theology* has the more modest goal of presenting theological analysis of specific issues in more limited contexts.

- Many today argue for theology that is culturally indigenous and sociologically contextual. The result is unparalleled theological pluralism.

For Further Reading and Reflection

Helpful introductions to biblical study include the following:

Grant, Robert H. *A Short History of the Interpretation of the Bible.* New York: Macmillan, 1963. This is an older work that needs to be tracked down in libraries or as a used book. But it is worth it. It is a substantive book about the varying ways scripture has been interpreted down through the centuries. It is written in an interesting, easily read style. It's major limitation is that it does not deal with the more recent kinds of biblical interpretation, including what has been happening in Roman Catholic circles since Vatican II.

Powell, Mark Allan. *What Is Narrative Criticism?* Minneapolis: Fortress Press, 1990. Powell picks up this more recent history with particular attention to the pattern named in the title of his book. He is thorough and sets out the material in a clear and orderly way.

Stuart, Douglas. *Old Testament Exegesis: A Primer for Students and Pastors,* 2d ed., revised and enlarged. Philadelphia: Westminster Press, 1984; and its companion volume: Fee, Gordon D. *New Testament Exegesis: A Handbook for Students and Pastors.* Louisville: Westminster John Knox Press, 1993. These books are designed to help students do the concrete work of exegeting, that is, explaining the meaning of biblical passages.

Tiffany, Frederick C., and Sharon H. Ringe. *Biblical Interpretation: A Roadmap.* Nashville: Abingdon Press, 1996. This is another careful and readable survey of recent trends in biblical interpretation. An interesting feature is an extensive interpretation of five biblical texts—three from

the Hebrew scriptures, two from the New Testament—
that uses these methods and shows their outcomes.

A helpful introduction to philosophy written in plain English for persons without background who want a broad overview and not a detailed presentation is:

> Solomon, Robert C. *The Big Questions: A Short Introduction to Philosophy*, 3d ed. New York: Harcourt Brace Jovanovich, 1982. Solomon has an engaging style, uses good illustrations, covers the main bases—including a brief history of Western philosophy, and even has a glossary of important philosophical terms at the end of the book.

I suggest that you review the exercise in epistemology that I set out above with some other theology students. Let someone try to argue each case and demonstrate the truthfulness of the assertion. Let someone else play devil's advocate and see how the proofs that are offered can be challenged. After working through the five statements that are provided, examine the statement "God is real." How do the justifications that are offered parallel or differ from those used for the other statements.

The fact that we all have operating epistemology, that is, a functioning sense of what it means to know something is the case, shows how philosophy can have relevance for theology. An important philosophical influence in contemporary American and British philosophy is a study of the functions of language. Rather than fussing with questions of ultimate reality, it has a more limited goal. It wants to be clear about the ways in which we assert claims to the truth and the parallel ways we can know not only how to demonstrate such assertions but if we can even legitimate that what we are saying makes any sense at all. Some statements give information. Others express feelings. Still others command. What kind of language is expressed in religious statements? What do you think is its particular function?

Begin to become aware of your own metaphysical assumptions. You can do this if you compare your responses to the following questions with those of others. How do you think God acts in the world? How can we know whether or not it is God that is at work? Do you assume that God directly intervenes in events? Why or why not? If you believe God works through miracles, what is the evidence? And how is this to be related to God's working in everything all the time? Or do you believe God lets the universe run on its own?

How do you respond to dogmatics and apologetics as two different strands of Christian theology? The former sees the limits of human wisdom and intelligence in connection with understanding God, while the latter values human beings' attempts to understand the world for the task of theology. Can they intersect with each other? If you believe so, how? Or is this a clear distinction that calls for a choice? And if so, why? What are some of the implications of your response to these questions for your own study of theology?

6

Constructing Theology

The Local "Architect/Contractor"

We have finally reached the point where we are able to review how theology is carried out. By now it should be apparent that this review is not interested only in how full-time theologians in academic settings carry out their work. Their work is very valuable. They serve as sources of new insights and stimulus for the Christian community's wrestling with the meaning and implications of its faith. They also remind the community of its heritage and the ongoing relevance of the Bible and church tradition. They are the persons consciously engaged in articulating the normative meaning of the gospel.

But ultimately, academic theology must touch base with the local situation and guide the tasks of preaching and teaching and the self-shaping and self-direction of congregations. And it should be made accessible and relevant to the lives of Christian people who have no theological training. Consequently, theology, while being something that can be pursued by laity and even interested non-Christians, is something that, when all is said and done, is an important responsibility of the church's resident theologians. Someone once likened their theological task to the electrical transformers that sit in local neighborhoods taking the high-voltage electricity that is produced by power plants and reducing it to household current so it can run vacuum cleaners and illuminate light bulbs. Local pastors are the ones who are called and trained to take high-voltage academic theology and reduce it to insight and perspective that can shape the lives of the people touched by their ministries.

By saying this I don't mean to restrict the study of theology to the ordained any more than to full-time professionals. As we've already noted, theology can be of benefit to personal growth. And beyond that, the more laity become theologically aware and theologically involved, the more the concrete life and outreach of the church will benefit. Local congregational leaders, individual Christians witnessing to their faith, and nonordained delegates to meetings of church assemblies will have more insight if they are theologically literate. And knowledge of theology is particularly essential for all those involved in the educational ministries of the church. Even persons not belonging to the church may find it interesting to discover how Christians understand their religious life and faith.

There are two different ways of thinking about this. One believes that theology should "trickle down"; the other, that it should "percolate up." However, instead of setting these two approaches against one another as adversarial alternatives, it's more helpful to appreciate the particular concerns each approach has. Such sympathetic appreciation will assist our own attempts to construct "household current" theology.

The "trickle down" theory values the work of academic theologians and their predecessors in the venerable history of Christian theology. It doesn't help to rehearse once more the arguments for the value of intellectualizing that were advanced in earlier chapters. Let it suffice to say that, over against the anti-intellectualism of our culture, persons who have the natural ability to engage in abstraction and critical analysis can help all of us understand issues much more clearly. The natural abilities, special training, and scheduled time that professional theologians have been given equip them for very important service to the Christian community.

By being introduced to the study of theology and by becoming acquainted with something of the development of Christian thought and some of the more influential contemporary theological "schools" and thinkers, resident theologians gain important resources. They have available to them perspectives on the church's life and ministry that are both faithful and relevant. By depending on traditional and contemporary academic theology, Christian rabbis are exposed to resources that can undercut identifying the gospel with their own private opinions. They are provided with insight and appreciations they would never have on their own. This is important enough that it bears repeating: Ordained clergy need to become acquainted with and value the work of contemporary professional theologians and the rich theological heritage of the past. Only such dependence and appreciation will keep them from confusing the hope and claims of the gospel with their own idiosyncratic opinions.

On the other hand, there is appreciation for perspectives that "percolate up" from the experiences of concrete Christian communities. This is one of the major arguments being made by liberation theologies, initially by those that have come out of Latin America. They argue that theological reflection needs to have roots in engaged action (*praxis*). Only the life of caring involvement in the pain of the world can understand what the gospel is. Theology is always "the second act." It doesn't precede the ministry of the church but follows after it. And theology certainly has no importance in and of itself, even if it is a theology of liberation. Breadth and depth of understanding may be communicated "from above," but insight into how this understanding applies to specific situations percolates up "from below," that is, from engagement with life issues at the local level.

We need to remember that theology does not always spring from academic roots, just as we need to recognize that the faith of the church is reflected in more than theology. It is expressed in its hymnody and liturgy, its creation in past history both of new forms of ministry (such as nursing and social service) and of special forms of life (such as monasticism and mysticism). Similarly, theology has been created within varied settings outside the academic world. Gerald O'Collins observes, for example, "Thomas More, Dietrich Bonhoeffer and other Christian theologians did some of their finest work as prisoners writing for a tiny circle of relatives and friends."[1] Of course, we need to remember that More and Bonhoeffer—and liberation theologians as well—were also trained in academic theology. Both academic learning and insight born of life experience profitably inform each other.

All of this is relevant to the residential Christian rabbi because ultimately God's Word is one that addresses concrete situations. Latin American theologians, for example, listening to local parish priests, discovered how institutional poverty has dehumanized their parishioners and how present economic patterns in that region offer no expectation of change. These concrete conditions stimulated these academics to create a theology, a perspective, that expressed the meaning and hope of the gospel in a pointed and relevant way. And in turn, local parish priests sought the insight and reactions of small groups gathered regularly for Bible study, prayer, and reflection on life experience. In this way, these *base Christian communities*, as they are called, have found guidance from the theology crafted by academics. But importantly and at the same time, they have been able to provide theologians with feedback and modifications that grow out of their continuing experience.

As we noted a while back, a parallel process is at work among Christian theologians who have been deeply affected by the woman's movement. The recognition of the patriarchal nature of our culture, the negative effects it has had on women and men, and its connection to our culture's attempt to dominate nature have awakened Christians to the presence of patriarchy in prior church life and in scripture.

---

[1] "Dogmatic Theology," in *The Westminster Dictionary of Christian Theology*, Alan Richardson and John Bowden, eds. (Philadelphia: Westminster Press, 1983), 164.

This has raised a major controversy in academic theology concerning the place of experience in constructing theology, something we will come back to later in this chapter. In the nineteenth and early twentieth centuries there was a lot of enthusiasm for seeing the presence of God in the movements connected to political, social, and economic transformation. Links were made between these movements of reform and the witness of the prophets and Jesus' witness to the reign of God. But some began to suspect that this was identifying God's Spirit and the human spirit too closely. They saw the danger of idolatry, that is, of seeing God as a reflection of ourselves, of making God in *our* image. The rise of the Nazi movement and the attempt of many pastors and theologians in Germany to connect it to the Bible and the Christian gospel seemed to illustrate exactly this point. As a result, much theology in this century has been suspicious of experience as a formative factor in theology and has instead insisted that God's self-disclosure in Jesus and the history of Israel is an unexpected, even alien, Word that establishes itself uniquely.

But theology doesn't sit still because life doesn't either. Even though there is widespread appreciation for this criticism and for an insistence on the unparalleled nature of God's communication of the divine will and nature, there is an increasing reaffirmation of the importance of insight born of powerful, life-healing, and life-transforming experiences. Latin American liberation theology, African American liberation theology in the United States, and feminist theology are important examples.[2] But there are other expressions as well. For those who don't believe that theology has any relevance for the actual life of Christian communities, I'd like to tell you briefly about the unique ministry that has been created by one of my former students. In her own personal journey she found a need for emotional healing and inner transformation. The work she did in therapy was supplemented by active participation in a twelve-step recovery program. The impact of this recovery was so powerful that she

---

[2]Readings that introduce these important forms of theology will be found at the end of this chapter.

felt compelled to sit down and figure out how it connected with traditional Christian teaching and insight. And in doing so, she let the one inform and critique the other. In other words, she set about constructing theology herself. But she didn't do it alone.

The constructive process began during her seminary studies. She read extensively, tried out ideas, argued cases, and listened to others' responses. She did this for her own spiritual benefit. She hungered to discover and name inner connections between two redemptive forces in her life—life in Christ and twelve-step recovery. She became a diligent student of biblical studies, systematic theology, depth psychology, and the outlines of recovery. And out of this process came a perspective that she believed was a *Christian* theology, not just a private one. It spoke to and on behalf of the community and suggested a unique form of ministry to her.

Marshaling her theological arguments, she gained the support of her denomination and founded a congregation specifically designed for persons in twelve-step recovery. The theological perspective she created helped her develop forms of congregational life and modifications of traditional liturgy that speak meaningfully—and powerfully—to these people. The results are not idyllic or uniform. Her mission congregation has had its problems, and some of them are connected with issues that recovering people bring with them. But this particular form of church life, mission, and ministry has brought persons into the church who otherwise would have remained alienated dropouts or skeptical unbelievers. And the effect of her work has grown beyond that congregation. A major theological press has published a collection of her sermons.[3]

This particular case demonstrates a number of things. First, there is a need for theology in the life of the church. Insightful perspective makes things happen. Second, theology needs to be informed by the rich heritage of the

---

[3]Michele S. Matto,*The Twelve Steps in the Bible* (New York: Paulist Press, 1991). If you have access to this book, you might want to read these sermons and see how they reflect her constructive integration of scripture, traditional doctrine, and insights found in twelve-step recovery.

past. Her theology and ministry have been saved from superficiality and "fad-ism" because both are deeply grounded in church tradition. Third, theology needs to come alive in local situations. It needs to take on concrete flesh and blood. Fourth, theology is always a communal enterprise. Those who dare to speak for the church need to hold themselves answerable to what has been said in the past and what is being said by others today. Theology requires the humility of conversation and dialogue. Fifth, theology is never finished. Personal and corporate history continually confronts us with new situations. Life experience that seems to resonate with something of the presence and impact of God needs attending to. Finally, because theology needs to be worked out at the local level, the persons who have this responsibility are those who have it given to them in their ordination.

Building Materials

By now the varying materials that are used to construct theology have been touched on in one way and to one degree or another. We only have to name them and perhaps provide an additional comment or two.[4]

Scripture

Throughout the history of Christian theology, the most important material for constructing theology has been *scripture*. The Protestant Reformation particularly made the scriptural witness to Christ the primary source and the working criterion or norm of the church's doctrine. And the papacy has recognized the essential authority of scripture as well. In the earlier part of this century, Pope Pius XII decreed that no one should interfere with the work of Roman Catholic biblical scholars. That decision resulted in the reforms of the Second Vatican Council, which were shaped in large measure by the work of these scholars. At no time since the Reformation have Roman Catholic and Protestant theologians had such a common understanding of the

---

[4]I have taken the listing of these basic construction materials from John Macquarrie's *Principles of Christian Theology*, rev. ed. (New York: Charles Scribner's Sons, 1977), 4–18. Follow up this introduction and see how Macquarrie treats these subjects in greater detail.

foundational character of the Bible. It is bedrock because it brings us more closely than anything else can to Jesus and the Jewish context out of which he came. It has reached a point where the work of Roman Catholic and mainstream Protestant and evangelical conservative Protestant biblical scholars is highly coherent, even interchangeable. They depend on and appreciate one another's work.

Having said that, there are significant differences in the ways theology uses this resource. For some, scripture is used *exclusively*. Any and all questions, from the Christian view of abortion to the practice of ordaining women, are answered by searching the pages of the Bible. For others, scripture is used *normatively*. Theology finds helpful resources outside the Bible but feels constrained to demonstrate that assertions that go beyond scripture are nevertheless coherent with the core of Hebraic and primitive Christian faith. Centrally, theological assertions must be tested by the criterion of Christ witnessed to by scripture. Still others use scripture *initially*, that is, scripture is important, since it is our only means of access to the origins of Christian faith and life. It comprises both the writings the primitive community itself deemed sacred (the Hebrew scriptures) and the writings produced by this community that became treasured by immediately succeeding generations (the New Testament). But these writings reflect their historical and cultural limitations. So although theology is respectful of them, it is free to move beyond them when new historical and cultural circumstances warrant.

It is not necessary to say much else. This is not because this source of theology is not important, but the very opposite. There is widespread agreement that everything the church teaches, proclaims, is, and does is grounded in the self-understanding of Israel and of the primitive Christian community as these are reflected in the scriptures. It is *the* irreplaceable resource for theology.

Revelation

But at the heart of theology's dependence on scripture lies a recognition of something more fundamental than the

Bible itself. It is the acknowledgment of *revelation*, of God's self-communication. Behind scripture are the experiences of persons who believed they had been presented with the disclosure of something that up until that moment had been either obscure or totally hidden. It is no accident that the Latin root for the English word *revelation* and its Greek equivalent both mean "an unveiling." Persons claim to have experienced revelation when they believe that they have been confronted with a specific or totally novel disclosure about God that God has initiated.

Classical theology usually interprets revelation as the disclosure of divine teachings by no one less than God. What are revealed are propositional truths that tell us things about God that the reach of human reason cannot discover. For example, Thomas Aquinas presents rational arguments that demonstrate that God exists. But, he argues, we need the special revelation of Christ witnessed to in the scripture to know that God is triune. This propositional understanding of revelation is still found among Roman Catholic, Lutheran, and Calvinist traditionalists and among fundamentalists. However, contemporary ecumenical theology, influenced by recent biblical studies, understands revelation to be the disclosure of God's presence, will, and meaning. Because God is the ultimate foundation and goal of life, this self-disclosure is also tantamount to the communication of the ultimate meaning of human existence. But such an interpretation agrees with the classical view in assuming that revelation occurs only through the will and activity of God and must be distinguished from all natural human capacities for discovery or insight.

In the Hebrew scriptures, divine disclosure is sometimes depicted as occurring through dreams and visions or through natural events. But more generally it is portrayed as special experiences that religiously sensitive persons have. It is as if something were being *said* to them. Sometimes these experiences of encountering God's self-disclosure are visionary, a kind of indirect communication. It is as if persons can see God's hand at work in events of personal or communal history. But the metaphor that is used refers primarily to sound, not sight. God's revelation is spoken of as a "word," as if the silence of God's otherness is bridged when God "speaks" to specially chosen or faithful persons such as the prophets. At the same time, this dominant Hebraic reference to God's communication through varying expressions of "word" is supplemented by references to "wisdom." Divine disclosure is linked to the implicit wisdom that governs the natural world and, even more importantly, the harmonious flow of human affairs. Looking closely at this pattern of harmony, one can see God's presence and will. Israel comes to know God, to experience the lifting up of the veil that hides God from our sight, when God communicates through the divine word or the divine wisdom

The New Testament builds on this earlier tradition. But the most decisive difference is its identification of the divine communication, God's word and God's wisdom, with the very person of Jesus Christ. Revelation is found not simply in Jesus' teaching but in the very nature of his life and action. His interaction with others, his responses to events, and especially his death and resurrection are the word of God "made flesh," as the gospel of John puts it. This explains why scripture is valued as much as it is. It is the best means of access to the fullness of God's self-disclosure in the person of Jesus.

Therefore, without identifying revelation with the Bible as much as fundamentalism does, this theological perspective closely links the two. Scripture is *witness literature*, testimony to occasions when persons believed themselves touched by God, and for the New Testament, particularly in and through Jesus. Even though the written expressions of the primitive church's recollection of Jesus and its evaluation of him date from several decades after Christ, they are irreplaceable witnesses to God's revelation in and through him. By doing this, they provide theology with the central criterion by which to evaluate church teaching.

Tradition

It has been customary for Roman Catholic and Protestant theology to divide over the question of the role of *tradition* in constructing theology. But recent decades have seen much convergence on this question. The major reason is a reframing of what *tradition* entails. Earlier, Roman Catholics had appealed to elements of church teaching and practice that have no biblical support but that had fairly early precedents. Examples would be the supremacy of Peter among the apostles as the basis for the institution of the papacy, the veneration of Mary and legendary accounts of her childhood and death, the devotion to the saints, and belief in purgatory. All of this Protestants rejected because of lack of any biblical support.

But today the role of tradition as a resource for theology is being approached differently. In the first place, scripture itself is seen more and more as the expression of the life of Israel and the early church, not of divine dictation. Therefore, there is great interest in learning as much as possible about these communities and their development. Other written materials outside the biblical canon and even relevant non-Jewish and non-Christian historical materials are deemed helpful in reconstructing a picture of them. We might say that biblical analysis no longer takes place in a spatial vacuum. Materials that are available from surrounding sources are helpful supplements.

Even more importantly, Protestants no longer approach scripture in a temporal vacuum. Recognizing momentous shifts in historical and cultural settings between the present and the biblical past, they have become interested in seeing how the church has always reappropriated the past from changing vantage points. Understanding how this has occurred in prior generations, and seeing the contributions developing traditions have made (and especially how they have subtly influenced contemporary church life and thought), become an important part of constructing theology. To put it differently, theology is shaped by acknowledging the dynamic character of church's history and appreciating the insights that have emerged after its beginnings.

Certain denominations are more indebted to tradition than others because they have an attachment to specific elements of past history. Roman Catholics, Eastern Orthodox, and many Anglicans pay careful attention to the work of "church fathers," that is, major teachers in early centuries of Christian history. Lutherans not only have deep appreciation for Martin Luther, but they also have held themselves accountable to their sixteenth-century confessional writings and have treasured a rich tradition of subsequent theological development. The same holds true, though to a lesser degree, for Calvinists. It is found, although more in the form of a general outlook than in specific historical documents, in the Wesleyan churches and their unique traditions. But even in cases of churches that have no official confessional documents or self-conscious tradition, they too have a well-developed and deeply appreciative memory.

Experience

One of the most significant and controversial factors in constructing theology is *experience*. This includes personal and communal experience and experience that is not only explicitly but also implicitly religious. The example just provided of a pastor's theological reflection on her own participation in twelve-step recovery illustrates how personal experience can be a significant factor in shaping theology. And we've noted how sharing in the experience of economic and social oppression endured by their underclass parishioners stimulated Latin American clergy and then theologians to create liberation theology. Here the experience that shaped theology was communal and societal, not just individual and personal.

But these two illustrations also demonstrate that the religious power and meaning of experience are not limited to what we usually understand "religious" experience to mean. Certainly, experiences of personal conversion or communion with God can have theological consequences. We only have to think of Paul to see how much his own conversion shaped his theology. He did nothing to merit connection to Christ. On the contrary, he was opposed to Jesus and his influence, and he persecuted the church. Consequently, Paul's encounter with the risen Lord was the clearest expression of God's unmerited grace, the acknowledgment of which was the cornerstone of his theology. Luther's discovery and personal appropriation of this Pauline teaching shaped his own theological articulation of the gospel.

But experience can be religious in another sense. Whenever persons undergo an experience that touches the very depths of their lives, transforming and healing them, claiming and motivating them, they sense they have been touched by God. The initial examples referred to earlier are cases in point. The inner struggle to reach greater measures of emotional health and the political struggle to resist the dehumanization of people can be encounters with the holy. Something of God's presence and meaning are believed to make themselves known. It is interesting to see how the theoretical work of Martin Luther King, Jr., in his doctoral work at Boston University, anticipated his later involvement in the civil rights struggle. But it is equally interesting to see how his being drawn into the experience of concrete political engagement gave new shape and intensity to his theology.

The question is, Just how influential should religious experiences be in the construction of theology? This is one of the most important issues being debated in contemporary theology and is the occasion for many deep disagreements. Without question, these experiences have great personal significance for those who are touched by them. That's because they are experienced as encounters with God. But should they be given a weight equal to scripture or even tradition? Put even more radically, is the shaping significance of personal or social religious experience equal to or greater than reference to Jesus? Is such experience the equivalent of "revelation"? And is there any guarantee that intense religious experience really expresses encounter with God? The enthusiastic identification of God's will with the Nazi program on the part of the so-called German Christian movement and the bloated corpses of suicide victims in Jonestown should make us exceedingly cautious about assuming that intense religious experience automatically carries weight.

Some want to restrict revelation to the past, or at least make all religious claims answerable to their ability to show coherence with the self-communication of God given in Jesus Christ. Others believe that, without denying the central importance of Jesus, there is need to take with deep seriousness the reality of the Holy Spirit. The Spirit is not restricted to the past but is alive and active today. Significantly, the gospel of John has Jesus refer to the Spirit who "will guide you into all the truth" (16:13). The implication seems to be that the disciples will not understand the fullness of God's truth even in their encounter with Jesus. But the counter-argument asserts that all claims as to what is and isn't the Spirit are answerable to the criterion of God's self-disclosure in Jesus Christ. This is reflected in that very same New Testament passage, which has Jesus say about the Spirit, "he will glorify *me*, because he will take what is *mine* and declare it to you" (16:14; italics added).[5]

But even if there is no agreement about the degree of significance that should be attached to experience, there is little question that it always plays some role in the way theology is constructed, sometimes greater and sometimes lesser.

Culture

Another element that goes into the construction of theology is the recognition of how our participation in the life of a particular culture or in a specific historical era deeply affects us, most usually at an unconscious level. This factor of *cultural and historical particularity* is one that has only been recognized in the last several centuries of Christian theology. Up until then, persons assumed that their outlook on things was fairly uniform and unchanging. This is indirectly reflected, for example, in the paintings of the nativity that were created in the medieval and Renaissance periods of Western history. The holy family, shepherds, and wise men are depicted wearing the style of clothing that was in fashion at the time of the painter, and Bethlehem looks not only like a city of their day but even of the particular region of Europe from which the painter came. In part this custom may well

---

[5]This is where feminist theologians who are self-consciously *Christian* differ from those who, like Mary Daly, have rejected the Christian church—and even Christ—as being hopelessly entangled in patriarchy. Christian feminists feel the claims both of their Christian roots and the transforming impact of feminist insight. Sometimes this creates powerful tensions, but the deciding issue is: What is it that establishes the final criteria, the organizing center, of theology?

express the painter's intention to make the nativity a contemporary event, much like a modern artist who depicts the holy family as African Americans glimpsed through the window of a tenement apartment house, with elements of an elevated subway track in the picture. But the unconscious factors in this style of painting go deeper. People usually assumed that life in Roman-occupied Palestine was pretty much the same as it was in early and late medieval Europe.

But the age of exploration and the development of modern scholarship that developed out of the Renaissance changed all that. Persons in Europe, and now in more and more parts of the world, have discovered the varieties of human self-understanding that not only span the globe but also continue to develop and change in history. Theologically, this means that as we become aware of these differences, we need to be conscious of their implications.

John Macquarrie writes, "Recognition of the cultural factor is equivalent to acknowledging that there is no final theology." The theologies that we have received from the past and even the writings of the Hebrew scriptures and the New Testament are all historically and culturally delimited. Today we have different assumptions about the nature of reality and the rational foundations for making truth claims. For this reason, it is argued, we must think through and express the meaning of the Christian faith in a way that is appropriate to our own time. Macquarrie warns that we must face this cultural component consciously and responsibly. We can't avoid it. "If we try to exclude this factor," he cautions, "then it will work unconsciously, for it is inescapable."[6]

There is a powerful illustration of Macquarrie's point in the way in which Protestant fundamentalists read scripture. They insist on the literal truth of each and every biblical passage, except in the obvious cases where metaphor or poetry is used. At the same time, they criticize modern biblical scholarship for selling out to "secular humanism" and its denial of biblical truth. The irony in all this is, it is *they* who have sold out to secular humanism. This intellectual movement is

---

[6]Macquarrie, 14–15.

also known as the Enlightenment or rationalism. It helped to create modern society, particularly American civilization. It is responsible for insisting on the freedom of individual conscience, unrestricted questioning of any and all traditional authority, and especially need for rational demonstration of the truth.

This cultural spirit was revolutionary and undermined the vestiges of medieval culture, including unquestioning obedience to the church. But in the process it also questioned the value of the Bible because it was not based on scientifically defensible fact or on rationally cogent arguments. It might express certain ethical wisdom, but it packages morality in legends, myths, and appeals to the supernatural. Beyond that, it was argued, the scriptures have no value. Moreover, they are unnecessary, since moral wisdom can be even more clearly discerned through rational reflection. At best, the Bible teaches morality to the uneducated masses.

Needless to say, this produced a powerful defense of the Bible on the part of theologians. However, in opposing what was often a very superficial and limited understanding of scripture on the part of these critics, some of the defenders bought into rationalistic epistemological assumptions. These assumptions included the notion that the only reliable kind of truth there is is *factual* truth, the truth that science can provide. If something is factual, it is true. The Bible is not factual, therefore it is not true.

But in responding, fundamentalists then and now do not challenge this epistemological assumption because they are unaware of the unconscious ways they themselves are shaped by culture. Being unaware, they cannot see how limited this assumption is. Instead they argue that the Bible is true because it *is* factual. Events in the Bible are not the events of ordinary history and not the workings of nature. They are events of divine history and the workings of God's supernatural power. But nevertheless, the Bible presents *facts* and, as Enlightenment epistemology implies, *that* makes it true.

The alternative response taken by nonfundamentalist theologians is to challenge these epistemological assumptions. As our brief epistemological exercise in chapter 4 tried to demonstrate, factual truth is *one* form of truth; scientific knowledge reflects *one* way of knowing. Human recognition of the truth about the world and about being human is much richer than acknowledging facts. And ironically, twentieth-century science is more modest about claiming to present such "facts" than the eighteenth-century epistemology that fundamentalism unwittingly accepts. Being conscious of cultural factors can help theology take up the question of the nature of truth and knowledge differently today and to see the limited nature of insisting on "facts" as the standard of truth. And that is the irony. Because it is insensitive to the cultural element in theology, fundamentalism is the unwitting victim of the epistemology of the very secular humanism it fulminates against.

Reason

The other major source of theological construction that has been touched on in a variety of ways is that of *reason*. We have looked extensively at the ways in which theology is a rational discipline. But we have also seen that the shape of such rationality can be expressed differently.

As we've already seen, theology often makes use of wide ranges of scholarship and insight. Learning something about the workings of human personality and interpersonal relationships, understanding social and political dynamics, and gaining insight into the spirit of an indigenous culture can be useful resources. Imagine for a moment how the communication of God's grace can be aided by even a rudimentary knowledge of depth psychology, family systems theory, or understanding the processes of addiction. Or think of the ways in which serving God's promise of the ultimate victory of God's kingdom can be correlated with the political struggles and spiritual exhaustion of marginalized people.

The resources created by human reason, which are the insights produced by many different academic disciplines, can serve constructive theology. But a major question is whether or not the discipline of philosophy should be used.

Here we face the potential use of reason in a second, more delimited sense.

We have noted that philosophical theology has looked to particular philosophical traditions or systems for clarity and direction in dealing with epistemology and metaphysics. Its reasons are far from arbitrary. Because God is the creator of all that is, God is the ultimate foundation of the human capacity to investigate and speculate on the nature of things. And the stimulus to seek the truth comes from God. Therefore, Christian theology should be encouraged to accept philosophy, like all other expressions of human creativity, as the gift of God and use it in God's service. This is perhaps the formative factor that is the most remote for beginning students of theology. Therefore, it might be worthwhile to spend a bit of time exploring how it is still shaping contemporary Christian self-understanding.

One of the most important contemporary expressions of the tradition of philosophical theology today, one found especially in the American theological circles, is called *process theology*. It is indebted to the reflections of two philosophers.

After a distinguished career as a mathematician at Cambridge University in England, Alfred North Whitehead arrived at Harvard to teach philosophy. More particularly, Whitehead advanced his own philosophical ideas, which posited a metaphysics that reflected the emerging understanding of reality in modern physics. This outlook understands that the fundamental character of the universe and its components is more akin to happenings or events than to things. In this context Whitehead found philosophical grounds to argue for the reality of God. This was quite a surprise. In the first place, it flew in the face of both the widespread popular assumption that religion and science are incompatible and the dominant philosophical assumption that metaphysics is dead. It also expressed a marked contrast to Whitehead's earlier religious views. Even though he had grown up as the son of an English clergyman, he had been basically agnostic. His philosophical reflections changed that.

The central argument that Whitehead makes is that the reality of God is necessary in order to understand how the universe can reflect stability and order and, at the same time, be fundamentally an unending process of transformation that allows for the inbreaking of radical novelty. Perhaps the most important element of this view of God is the argument that rather than being the chief exception to how the universe operates, God, the very foundation of the universe's unfolding existence, is the chief expression of these operations. In a sense, therefore, God is finite, but not simply as everything else is. As the expression of love, God is self-limiting in establishing and affirming the reality of the universe and in being affected by it, moving the universe not through force but through persuasion.

Whitehead's ideas were developed by an American philosopher, Charles Hartshorne, who served as his assistant at Harvard. Hartshorne spoke of "the divine *relativity*," which contrasts with the traditional Greek assumption that God's perfection is coextensive with being complete, self-contained, and therefore unchangeable. Hartshorne argues that God's perfection is different. The classical understanding of divine perfection holds true in one sense. It applies *abstractly* to God, who grounds the full range of possibilities as to how things can be. But God is also *concrete*. And in this respect, God interacts with the universe and is affected by it. This means, for example, that although God always abstractly knows everything that can be possibly known, God's concrete knowledge changes as the world changes. This doesn't mean that as the universe develops God becomes wiser. But it does mean that as the universe expresses real novelty in its evolutionary unfolding, God and God's knowledge are enriched.

Perhaps only this brief glimpse[7] of process theology can give you clues why it has become very closely tied to dialogue between science and religion, to concern about the environment and the future of the planet, and to feminist

---

[7] For a helpful overview of process theology and an introductory bibliography, see the entry by David Ray Griffin under this heading in *A New Handbook of Christian Theology*, edited by Donald W. Musser and Joseph L. Price (Nashville: Abingdon Press, 1992). Also note Griffin's brief overview of the work of one of the leading process theologians, John B. Cobb, Jr., in *A Handbook of Christian Theologians*, enlarged edition, edited by Martin E. Marty and Dean G. Peerman (Nashville: Abingdon Press, 1989).

theology's insistence on the nonauthoritarian nature of God. Because it believes God is a reality in the life of *every* person and is the most deeply relevant factor in the creative transformation and healing of life *universally*, it is not surprising that process theology is open to dialogue with non-Christian religions.

As you can see, process theology's appreciation of a novel metaphysics closely aligned with the modern scientific reading of the natural world is a major example of a contemporary philosophical theology. But its critics charge that not only does it argue against the prevailing *philosophical* opinion that metaphysics is illegitimate, but it also might be a case of the tail wagging the dog. Isn't there a danger that the God of process theology owes more to Whitehead and Hartshorne than it does to scripture and church tradition? Process theologians argue that it connects better to these resources than other options. For example, it makes a kind of sense out of the references in the Hebrew scriptures to God's mind being changed, and it can make metaphysical sense out of the fundamental affirmation in Johannine writings that, at rock bottom, God *is* love. And, they argue, it does so while at the same time taking seriously the vision of reality given in quantum physics, emergent evolution, and contemporary awareness of the importance of history.

Although, as process theology illustrates, philosophical theology is alive today, it is not the dominant or unchallenged player in the field. We have already noted how other theological systems consciously avoid dependence on philosophy. Once again, the reasons have been thoughtful ones. Synthesis with philosophy, it is argued, produces a theology shaped too much by human judgments and too little by divine revelation, which transcends human reason. The radical uniqueness of the Christian gospel becomes tailored to fit philosophical knowledge. Even more problematically, philosophical theology fails to recognize the radical nature of sin, which corrupts even the greatest of human achievements, including philosophy. Sin distorts the human soul, the human spirit, and the human mind. Therefore, theology must depend solely on God's self-communication and must be independent from philosophy.

What is interesting to note, however, is that both the proponents and the opponents of philosophical theology present carefully reasoned cases. And if we are to evaluate what they assert, then we will have to examine their arguments by using critical thinking. This implies that theology is linked to human rationality in still a third sense, namely, the process of rational evaluation. Using critical thinking means we will have to review and critique the assumptions these conflicting positions make. And we will have to see whether the progression of their arguments is logical and whether the conclusions they draw from their premises are valid. So even if theology does not want to use philosophy or even other rational disciplines such as psychology or sociology, it still must use disciplined reasoning.

Developing a Blueprint

The most crucial issue for constructing theology is that of *method*, as it is called. *Which* resources should we use? *How* should we use them? And which have *priority*?

If you look back at the examples I have provided of the alternative ways for approaching aspects of theology, you will see that the differences between them are all differences in method—insistence on restricting theology to dogmatics, and openness to apologetics. The long-standing Roman Catholic appeal to tradition, and the long-standing Protestant rejection of it. The concern to have theology percolate up from below, and the pursuit of philosophical theology. The use of scripture by fundamentalists, and the appeal to life-transforming experience by feminist theologians. Holding oneself answerable to the theology of the church fathers, and seeking one that is indigenously Asian.

Note that differences can cut across many lines. It is possible for someone to construct an Asian feminist theology that might, oddly enough, show deep appreciation for some particular church "father" or perhaps build on the Reformation tradition of what is called "the theology of the cross." But in each case, basic differences between concrete expressions of theology result from differences in method. It is method that determines which building materials will be picked out and how they will be used. It is the blueprint used in constructing theology.

Because of the increasing numbers of methods that are being used today and the disparity between them, beginning students might be tempted to throw up their hands in confusion and resignation. Why bother to study theology at all if there is no theological agreement and theologians believe they have strong arguments for their interpretations of the Christian faith?

If theology were just a private enterprise, then entering this discussion might prove stimulating for some but would still be unnecessary. But we've said that theology is a *communal* discipline carried out by the Christian community for the sake of its witness, mission, and ministry. Consequently, theology always takes the form of a conversation, even if at times the talk gets very loud and even belligerent. The danger is, given our own human frailty we tend to be defensive. We are self-justifying and engage in rationalization. That can be true even for the most learned and most pious theologian. Sadly, too often we perceive those holding differing points of view as adversaries who need to be attacked or avoided.

But what if we allowed our theology to be shaped not only by our inescapable vulnerability to sin but also our obedience to God? Then, even if we still had deep convictions and even though there still would be significant theological differences between us, there would be a different spirit about our interaction with each other.

- In the first place, we *would* interact. We wouldn't just cluster with those who thought the same way we did and indulge in mutual affirmation and long-distance potshots at others. We would find ourselves called to a life of respectful dialogue. We would be open to really listening to others.

- In the second place, we would still witness vigorously to what we believe are the claims that God has made on us, and we would embrace the requirement of debating our case. In fact, our being claimed by what we understand to be the truth of the gospel would be the particular vocation to which we believe we have been called and would represent the potential contribution we can make to the wider church and theological community.

- But, third, we would learn to express *humble* convictions that recognize we can be, and often have been, mistaken or at least limited in our understanding. Constructing theology before the cross of Christ calls us to embrace the principle of self-criticism. It means acknowledging that only God is absolute.

- And finally, even though the exchanges between us would be spirited and even sharp, we would dare to believe that God might be trying to speak to us through the witness of the other. Then the differences between us *might* not be conflicting alternatives but potential sources of enrichment.

Beyond the Labels "Liberal" and "Conservative"

Perhaps by this time you are beginning to sense the wide spectrum of theologies that are present within the Christian community today. By becoming more aware of them and the different methodological issues that are at stake, you should begin to recognize how simplistic it is to reduce the many shadings of this spectrum to a contrast between black and white. It is not the case that some theologies are "conservative" and others are "liberal." It's far more complicated than that.

The most important issue that has shaped theology over the last centuries has been the impact that the rise of the modern world has made on traditional theological authority. I've already touched on the challenges of modern methods of scholarship, modern science, the emergence of the epistemology of rationalism, the increasing influence of secularism, and the encounter with global cultural pluralism. These and other forces have questioned the reliability, or at least the unquestioned authority, of the traditional sources of theology. It has made the question of method central.

In the face of these challenges, theology has expressed three broad responses. The first of these, represented by

Roman Catholic and Protestant traditionalists, has been simply to find ways of neutralizing or ignoring these challenges and to reassert traditional authority. The second has been a tendency to embrace this new post-medieval culture and create a synthesis with it. This has resulted in certain kinds of philosophical theology, for example, religious movements like Deism and even separate church bodies like the Unitarian church. The third response, which came to be called *liberalism* in Protestant circles and *modernism* in Roman Catholic ones, has had a different strategy. It has embraced certain elements of modern culture and resisted others and has done so with the goal of safeguarding a special role for religion and for the Christian faith in particular. So be aware that when you come across references to "liberal theology," it has a very specific meaning, not the popular one.

Modern biblical scholarship is an example of this "liberal" approach. It not only accepted modern methods of historical and literary analysis, but more than any other factor in Western culture it was responsible for developing these methods. At the same time, it worked in tandem with philosophical theology to provide careful arguments for the truth of scripture by resisting the epistemological standards of rationalism. Theological liberalism aimed at creating a synthesis with modern culture in much the same way Thomas Aquinas sought a synthesis between the dominant theology of his day and the rediscovery of Aristotle's philosophy that happened through crusaders' encounters with the Arabs. Theological liberalism believed that by affirming the creations of the human spirit at its best—not only science and disciplined scholarship, but even more importantly, the realization of human rights and democratic institutions—it could wed them to a nonsupernatural "essence" of ancient Christian tradition.

Because theological liberalism was open to the spiritual achievements of modern culture, it relied on secular learning, it valued religious experience, and it tended to be selective about the elements of scripture and tradition it relied on. It sometimes became associated with what came to be called "the social gospel." This theological viewpoint saw the saving work of Jesus not so much as making propitiatory sacrifice for the sins of the world as transforming person's hearts and minds. The result was that such redeemed persons gave themselves to the establishment of a more just, humane, and improved world, that is, to the building up of the kingdom of God in this life.

This close alliance with the forces that shaped nineteenth-century European and North American culture began to shown strains at the end of the century and shattered with the collapse of cultural optimism that two world wars and worldwide economic depression brought on. Protests arose within the ranks of theological liberalism itself, leveled against its idealism and optimism, its too close identification of movements of political and social reform with the kingdom of God, and its failure to insist on the uniqueness of God's self-disclosure in Christ. Without abandoning commitment to modern scholarship or to social witness, this corrective movement found resources in traditional doctrines, even though they were reappropriated in fresh ways. For example, ancient biblical themes such as "the demonic," "idolatry," and corporate sin suddenly had relevance as these chastened liberals opposed fascist and communist totalitarianism. "The strange new world of the bible" (as Karl Barth—a major leader in this theological movement—phrased it) became the paramount resource for theology, as did the great historic tradition of the church, particularly the Reformation. It should come as no surprise, therefore, that this corrective movement that grew out of theological liberalism came to be known as *neo-orthodoxy*.

The results have been very interesting. The gulf that existed earlier between traditionalists on the one hand and theological liberals on the other became bridged, creating a major coalition of theological forces. Neo-orthodoxy continued to interact with culture, but did so in a prophetic stance that saw the kingdom of God critiquing the corporate sin embodied in unjust political and social systems. It used the methods of biblical scholarship, but in doing so saw the radical otherness of God's revelation in Christ criticizing human religion rather than simply confirming it. It continued to call the church to deep involvement in the world, but from the standpoint of the promises of God and the hidden activity of God in human history, not from one that identified the hand of God with tangible human progress. In this way, neo-orthodoxy attracted numbers of disillusioned theological liberals at the same time it gave traditionalists a road out of theological isolation and into the twentieth century. It became *the* dominating theological outlook of the middle third of the century, the core of an ecumenical theology that continues to cut across denominational lines and makes many Protestants and Roman Catholics feel closer to each other today than to their more tradition-oriented coreligionists.

What has been happening, however, in the last several decades is that neo-orthodoxy has been undergoing its own internal development. Some of the older perspectives of theological liberalism are reasserting themselves, although not in the same way they did earlier. The most important reassertion has to do with the role of experience in theological method. This *neo-liberalism,* if we can call it that, is open to religions other than Christianity and to the sorts of personal and social experience I mentioned earlier. It also traces out connections between certain liberation movements in history with the inbreaking of God's promises of the kingdom. Without abandoning neo-orthodoxy's reassertion of the power of sin in human affairs, it is interested in tracing connections between God's Spirit and certain movements of the human spirit—especially ethical commitment to peace, justice, and human rights. There are also theologies open to experiences as diverse as mysticism and personal psychological/spiritual growth.

Therefore, to speak of theologies being either "conservative" or "liberal" is too simplistic. Most theologies are conservative to one degree or another. They want to conserve, that is, preserve and treasure and be shaped by the rich resources of the past. They have *reverence* for the original roots of the Christian community. Looking at the first three sources

Constructing Theology 115

for constructing theology that were listed earlier—scripture, revelation, and tradition—you will see they have this general character. To the extent that theology draws on them, it will be "conservative."

And the word "liberal" comes from the Latin word *liber*, meaning "free." If we use the term loosely and not technically, then we can say theology that is liberal is "freed up" theology. It is theology that senses the presence and movement of God in the wider reaches of the world outside the church and in the nearer reaches of the present. Most theologies are liberal to one degree or another in their concern to appreciate the ongoing *relevance* of the gospel. And if you review the latter three sources that we have noted—experience, culture, and reason—you will see they reflect this concern.

Therefore, when you begin to study theology and encounter different systems or schools or individual theologians, resist your temptation to pigeonhole them as "liberal" or "conservative." Instead, try to understand the ways they attempt to be *both* reverent *and* relevant and what sort of blueprint they use in constructing their interpretation of the meaning of Christian faith and life out of the materials that are available.

Moreover, you will find that differences in theological method also reflect the fact that theology is the "hybrid" discipline we have already explored briefly. It is carried out by the Christian community on behalf of its own internal needs and shaped by its own internal commitments, centrally to God's self-disclosure in Jesus Christ. At the same time, it is an academic discipline, using the methods of informed scholarship and disciplined thinking. All theologies will express their place within the life of the church to one degree or another. And there are degrees. But some theologies will understand themselves to be conversations that are public and academic in character more than others. These commitments to church and to academy are parallel to, but not identical with, the factors of reverence and relevance. How these pairs of concerns work themselves out should not be simplistically collapsed into "liberal" and "conservative" categories. Therefore, resist the temptation to evaluate theologies this way and, instead, learn to discern methodological differences.

Summary

- Academic theologians bring a breadth and depth of understanding to guide the life, mission, and ministry of the church. But ultimately their perspectives need to be applied to the life of concrete Christian communities by their resident theologians.

- Just as theology can inform the church's life, so too engagement in life issues, *praxis,* also profitably informs the work of theologians.

- In applying theology to local situations, resident theologians need to be informed by church heritage, be aware of concrete needs and issues arising in their ministry, and be part of a process of communal conversation.

- The building materials of theology include those that reflect "reverence" for the givenness of gospel—scripture, revelation, and tradition. Centrally, indebtedness to these resources expresses obedience and responsiveness to God's self-communication in Jesus Christ.

- Other building materials include those that reflect concern for "relevance" to the concrete human context of theology—culture, reason, and experience. Such indebtedness expresses the conviction that God is present and active in and through the Spirit.

- Theological "method" refers to the ways in which these various resources for theological construction are or are not used, how they are used, and the priorities they have.

- The increasingly different ways in which these potential resources are brought together has created an unparalleled number of theological methods. The basic goal of beginning theology students should be to discern these differing methods and understand what happens when they function in a context of engaged yet open dialogue.

- The varying responses of Christian theology to the challenges of the modern world cannot be reduced to a simple distinction between "conservative" and "liberal." The history of theology since the Enlightenment is rich and varied and produced not only traditionalist theologies resistant to it and a few unqualified endorsements of it, but also the more qualified responses of liberalism, neo-orthodoxy, and now "neo-liberalism."
- Theologies usually reflect in varying ways and to varying degrees both a commitment to conserve the foundations of Christian faith and life and an openness to address the needs and claims of the current historical situation. They also are shaped by commitments to both the church and the academy.

For Further Reading and Reflection

As we have seen, careful arguments can and have been made on both sides of the question of the role of experience in theology. It is perhaps the most contentious issue in current debates, although it reflects the many different sides of experience that theologians appeal to. Therefore, it is a good idea to start thinking through the issue even though you are only beginning to study theology. Can you see the potential problems that can result in appealing to experience? Can you sense advantages?

Everyone has an implicit method that operates for them, just as they have an inferred theology. Can you begin to identify your own way of approaching theological issues? What building materials are important to you, and why? Do you rule any out, and why? When it comes to different sources, which one or ones have priority, and why? Take some time to begin to think through these questions. Share your understanding with some other theology students and see how your reasons for substantiating your respective methods might influence one another.

The influence of experience on contemporary theology is expressed in a number of ways. Perhaps the most important are those theologies reflecting the impact of various dimensions of "liberation." I mentioned "liberation theology," which is more commonly called "Latin American liberation theology," since it has its origins there. However, there are now liberation theologies indigenous to other parts of the world. Another important strand is focused on the experience of African Americans. It is usually known as "black theology of liberation" or simply "black theology." A third major expression is the "feminist theology" I've mentioned that builds on the insights of the feminist movement. A subsection of this school is centered in the special struggles of African American women, who must deal with sexism and racism, and is distinguished from feminist theology more generally by being called "womanist theology."

For helpful profiles of liberation, black, feminist, and womanist theologies, see the entries under those names in Donald W. Musser and Joseph L. Price, eds., *A New Handbook of Christian Theology* (Nashville: Abingdon Press, 1992). Each entry also lists a helpful bibliography to open up the subject. In addition to the titles listed there, note the following:

Latin American and Third World Liberation Theology

Boff, Leonardo. *When Theology Listens to the Poor*. San Francisco: Harper & Row, 1988.

Brown, Robert McAfee. *Liberation Theology: An Introductory Guide*. Louisville: Westminster John Knox Press, 1993.

Ferm, Dean William. *Profiles in Liberation: 36 Portraits of Third World Theologians*. Mystic, Conn.: Twenty Third Publications, 1988.

Hebblethwaite, Margaret. *Base Communities: An Introduction*. Mahwah, N.J.: Paulist Press, 1994.

Jesudasan, Ignatius. *Ghandian Theology of Liberation*. Maryknoll, N.Y.: Orbis Books, 1984.

Pieris, Aloysius. *Asian Theology of Liberation*. Maryknoll, N.Y.: Orbis Books, 1988.

Black Theology

Cone, James. *God of the Oppressed*. New York: Seabury Press, 1975.

Hayes, Diana L. *And Still We Rise: An Introduction to Black Liberation Theology*. New York: Paulist Press, 1996.

Roberts, J. Deotis. *Liberation and Reconciliation: A Black Theology.* Maryknoll, N.Y.: Orbis Books, 1994.

———. *Black Theology in Dialogue.* Maryknoll, N.Y.: Orbis Books, 1990.

Feminist Theology

Carmody, Denise L. *Christian Feminist Theology.* Oxford/Cambridge, Mass.: Blackwell, 1995.

Grey, Mary. *Feminism, Redemption and the Christian Tradition.* Mystic, Conn.: Twenty Third Publications, 1990.

LaCugna, Cathrine Mowry, ed. *Freeing Theology: The Essentials of Theology in Feminist Perspective.* New York: HarperCollins, 1993.

McFague, Sallie. *Models of God: Theology for an Ecological, Nuclear Age.* Philadelphia: Fortress Press, 1987.

Ruether, Rosemary Radford. *Sexism and God-Talk: Toward a Feminist Theology.* Boston: Beacon Press, 1983.

Schüssler Fiorenza, Elisabeth. *In Memory of Her: A Feminist Theological Reconstruction of Christian Origins.* New York: Crossroad, 1984.

General and Cross-Referenced Liberation Theology

Anderson, Gerald H., and Thomas F. Stransky. *Liberation Theologies in North America and Europe.* New York: Paulist Press, 1979.

Chopp, Rebecca. *Praxis of Suffering: An Interpretation of Liberation and Political Theologies.* Maryknoll, N.Y.: Orbis Books, 1986.

Chung, Hyun Kyung. *Struggle to Be in the Sun Again: Introducing Asian Women's Theology.* Maryknoll, N.Y.: Orbis Books, 1990.

Cone, James H. *Speaking the Truth: Ecumenism, Liberation and Black Theology.* Grand Rapids: Eerdmans, 1986.

Cummings, George C. L. *Common Journey: Black Theology (USA) and Latin American Liberation Theology.* Maryknoll, N.Y.: Orbis Books, 1993.

Ruether, Rosemary Radford. *Liberation Theology: Human Hope Confronts American Power.* New York: Paulist Press, 1972.

Soelle, Dorothee. *The Window of Vulnerability: A Political Spirituality.* Minneapolis: Fortress Press, 1990.

Thistlethwaite, Susan Brooks, and Mary Potter Engles, eds. *Lift Every Voice and Sing: Constructing Christian Theologies from the Underside.* New York: Harper & Row, 1990.

7

Developing Skills in Critical Thinking

The word *critical* has surfaced several times, and we've looked briefly at the technical meaning it has in a variety of academic disciplines, including theology. Coming across the term, we tend to assume that being "critical" means finding fault or being disparaging. Or else we associate it with something that is urgent or crucial and needs immediate attention. But the technical use is closer to the original Greek roots of the word. In Greek, a *krites* was a judge who was thought to be *kritikos*, that is, discerning, capable of making wise distinctions in the cases brought before him. That's because he (and in those days they were all male) operated with good *criteria*, or standards of judgment. He was a judge who didn't simply look at the surface of things. Instead, he was able to probe beneath and *krinein*, that is, discern otherwise hidden agendas, connections, motives, and extenuating circumstances.

Theology, like all intellectual disciplines, calls for *critical thinking*.[1] This is thinking that is wise and discerning because

---

[1] Perhaps the most helpful review of the role of critical thinking in theology is presented by Howard W. Stone and James O. Duke in their book *How to Think Theologically* (Minneapolis: Fortress Press, 1996). A panoramic but highly technical

it is aware of how hidden presuppositions and assumptions shape assertions. It is thinking that knows how to make careful distinctions on the basis of valid standards of judgment. It is thinking that knows how to get beneath the surface and identify relevant issues. It is a special kind of thinking that people seldom discover outside the opportunities and demands encountered in advanced education. This is not to say that prehistoric peoples or contemporary cultures that do not have extensive systems of modern education, for example, lack critical thinkers in their populations. But it is the case that the percentage is much less than in situations where persons are challenged by the processes of formal education to develop critical thinking.

Education exposes us to wider ranges of experience than we could ever possibly have on our own. That's the constant miracle of reading books. In reading them, we are enriched by sharing the internal and external experience of many other persons. And if we are receptive to what we encounter, we can have our horizons expanded. But in order to profit most from our reading, we need to learn how to carry on a critical dialogue with the text. Education gives us increased measures of information and enables us to develop skills. Perhaps the most challenging and important of these skills is critical thinking.

I've already mentioned that the medieval church created the first liberal arts curriculum as the course of study that would best prepare persons for the priesthood. And the extensive system of liberal arts colleges established in the United States by churches very often began as institutions preparing persons for ordained ministry. One effect of such study was to give persons a broad background that could help them understand the human condition better. But another was to develop the capacity for critical thinking as helpful preparation for theological studies.

---

survey of relevant issues is found in Joanne G. Kurfiss, *Critical Thinking: Theories, Research, Practice and Possibilities,* ASHE-ERIC Higher Education Reports 2 (Washington, D.C.: Association for the Study of Higher Education, 1988). A less technical presentation developed for educators is Stephen D. Brookfield, *Developing Critical Thinkers* (San Francisco: Jossey-Bass Publishers, 1987).

The contemporary educational situation is much different. We've already noted that increasing numbers of persons studying theology today do not necessarily have a liberal arts course of study going on while or before they start that study. Consequently, many have not had encouragement in the classroom to develop critical thinking. But this needn't be an obstacle. Over the last several decades, research in developmental psychology has determined that critical thinking is a skill that can be learned. It's not something akin to an innate ability—like having perfect pitch or having exceptional motor coordination. Such skills are given to some and not others and give the lucky recipients an edge in being musicians or gymnasts. But critical thinking is something each of us can learn to one degree or another. In fact, your study of theology presents an opportunity for you to develop this skill.

What follows are some general observations about approaching the study of theology. The hope is that they may ease your path and help you maximize your efforts. Among these observations is a profile of how critical thinking develops. It may enable you to locate where you are in the process and understand at what points you will feel the challenges—and the frustrations—that come with facing potential growth. This may help you discover wider measures of patience and understanding for yourself, your instructors, the authors you are reading, and your fellow theology students, who may be at a point in the process that differs from your own.

A Point of Departure

In describing the process of constructing theology, in outlining its component elements, in raising the question of method, and in giving you a brief outline of some of the current issues that are shaping theology, I have exposed you to more than you can possibly begin to use at the beginning of your studies. You are hardly ready to start theological construction on your own. Doing that—in your own modest way—could be a long-range goal. More immediately, the profile you've been presented should help you understand how the authors you read go about their work.

The primary place to begin study of Christian theology is to get to know church teaching as widely and deeply as you can. In part this means coming to know something of how its major elements emerged in the history of the Christian community. And it means becoming acquainted with the shared catholic tradition that the greater portions of churches have in common. You can only understand contemporary theology if you understand what it presupposes. Therefore, read some introductions to Christian doctrine that discuss traditional topics (the classical *loci*, as we have noted) at an elementary level. Then read theologians that advance the conversation.[2]

Getting grounded in traditional teaching is especially important for those who are members of historically conscious churches that have a strong doctrinal tradition. Appreciating that heritage can provide a "gyroscopic center" in the midst of the dynamism and pluralism of the contemporary theological scene. If you can avoid being defensive or absolutistic about this heritage, it won't become a wall separating you from others. In fact, being grounded in a specific tradition can aid you in becoming open to contemporary challenges and ecumenical encounter. The more you feel grounded, the less confused and defensive you will be in meeting points of view that differ from your own. And the more you can faithfully and clearly represent your tradition, the more of a genuine contribution you can make to others as you engage in dialogue with them.

This immediate goal of becoming grounded is all the more important given the fact that large numbers of persons who begin studies in theology today have very limited church education. As a result, they have superficial and even confused notions about what the church teaches. The official or informed theology of the churches often is strikingly different from widespread popular impressions—even among some clergy!—and certainly is quite distinct from the general "religiousness" that is prevalent in American culture. Theology is not just private opinion but, as we have noted, it

---

[2]Bibliographical suggestions are given at the end of this chapter.

reflects the attempt of the Christian *community* to identify and express dimensions of what it believes. The traditional term for instruction in Christian doctrine is *catechesis*. The fact is, effective catechesis is at a low ebb. Some have estimated that the average church-goer has the equivalent of a third- to fifth-grade understanding of the Christian faith. Even many persons entering seminaries these days have little background in the church tradition into which they want to be ordained and sometimes are recent converts—even to Christianity itself![3] The sad state of theological affairs in the pews is even more reason for persons studying theology, especially if they are studying in order to assume leadership roles in the church, to take those studies seriously and work at them rigorously. It does not mean insisting that all others in a congregation have the same measure of theological understanding, but rather it implies that only those who have prepared themselves responsibly can provide *any* theological leadership.

Your initial study will also begin to acquaint you with some of the major issues and concerns that are shaping contemporary theological scholarship. This will be aided by including in your studies exposure to the history of theology over the past two centuries. Along the way you may well discover some particular debates or some special concerns that interest you, which you can pursue on your own. In the process, you may develop a deep interest in a particular expression of contemporary theology, such as an African-American theology of liberation or a particular philosophical theology. But you can best follow these narrower interests if you understand the wider landscape into which they fit.

If your study is going to be an extensive one rather than an introduction, if for example you are preparing for ministry within the church, then it may prove helpful for you to get to know the work of a major theologian or "school" of theology thoroughly. This could be a major figure from the distant past (like Augustine or Calvin) or near past (like Rahner or Barth) or the present (like liberation or feminist

---

[3]See footnote 3 on page 41.

theologians). If you are unaware of the broader contexts of theology, this specific focus could constrict you. But the advantage is that, like those who become grounded in their own traditions, you will have a "home base" with which you identify and from which you can move out into wider discussions.

You may also discover that the points of view or types of theology with which you identify will shift over time. The more we change, the more our thinking does as well. This certainly has been true for me. When I began my theological studies in seminary, I had passing contact with the work of a particular theologian. I was uninterested in pursuing this approach to theology at the time because, frankly, the level of his thinking was far beyond my reach, but also—and more importantly—I found what he said very intimidating. Later on, however, an aspect of his work became the subject of my doctoral dissertation, and today I am deeply influenced by his approach.

This transformation is parallel to my experience of going to an art museum during those seminary years and seeing the work of Spanish artist Joan Miró for the first time. I was outraged! I thought his paintings were inane, juvenile, ugly, worthless. Now he is one of my favorite twentieth-century painters, and I treasure the copy of one of his seriographs that I have in my home. What happened? Miró hadn't changed; I had. As I outgrew some of my own psychological constrictedness, some important measures of playfulness and psychic energy were released, which enabled me to recognize and deeply appreciate the exuberant childlikeness of Miró's very sophisticated work. We can grow into perspectives that used to confuse or threaten us. Don't be surprised if something like that happens to you in your study of theology.

The Challenge to Reach Out

These events in my own history illustrate the very point that developmental psychology has been making about our capacity to develop skills in critical thinking. For a number of years, I was baffled about what to say to students who found themselves foundering. They picked up theological texts, read every word on a page, knew that it was written in English, but ended up not understanding anything. Part of my advice to them I have already given to you: Don't overreach yourself and plunge right into advanced studies. Know that you are tuning in to conversations that have been going on for a long time. Understand that you are dealing with technical vocabulary and many nuances that are packed into a few words. Be patient with the authors (and forgive them when they write in "academese" and don't have you in mind at all). Most of all be patient with yourself—and persistent.

But I also knew that at certain times students were struggling not with the *content* of what they were reading but with the question of *how* to read and think about it. They hadn't learned how to carry on an ongoing "critical" dialogue with the text because they had limited skills in critical thinking. And all I could do is encourage them not be hard on themselves. A delimited capacity to think critically is not an indictment of anyone's intelligence. More often it reflects degrees of exposure and willingness to pursue the process.

I also encouraged them to share their difficulties with others, reach out in mutual support, and "keep hanging around" until one day they discovered that they "caught on" to thinking theologically. I likened it to learning to ride a bicycle: wobbling handlebars, pants legs caught in the chain and gears, skinned knees, and lots of discouragement. Then, one day, a sort of magic occurs and you "catch on," you find your balance, you "get it," and away you go!

I still think all of that is true. And certainly no one can work the process for you. But educational psychology can give us some notions about the direction of the process, the stages persons go through, and what will be faced along the way. It may not make difficulties disappear, but at least you can all know, first, that you are not alone in this; others share where you are either now or in the past. And, second, contrary to what you may be tempted to assume, your instructors and the authors that you read are not playing intellectual games or talking gibberish. Instead, they can see farther than you do. And that's what education is about. The confusion you may feel can be due to the fact that, for all their knowledge, they are not able to communicate with you at your level. Or it may be that they are intent on connecting with others where *they* are. There is a potential in you for more mature understanding that, even if it seems confusing or threatening, will blossom if you work for it. You have the capacity to become *wiser* and not just more informed—*if* you are willing to embrace change. The more permission and energy you give to your own growth, the more you will be able to help people in their own process. By moving into another stage yourself, you will be able to understand more than before.

What then is the overall direction of the process? It moves toward enabling persons to discover *and accept* a world that is much larger and more complicated than they thought it was. It helps persons be more open to new experience and new ways of seeing the world. It simultaneously affirms confidence and humility and thus enables persons to accept greater measures of ambiguity and uncertainty. It helps persons become more flexible and curious and in that way not only tolerate complexity but actually welcome it. Most of all, it spills far beyond the ways in which persons *think* and shapes the ways they *live*.[4]

When we offer resistance to this process, it is not because we are being irresponsible or arbitrary; we are not to be "faulted." The point is, because we want stability in our lives, we tend to integrate new experiences and understand new information in terms of what we *already* know or believe. It is hard for us to break out of these habitual ways so that we can see things, interpret experience, or take in information afresh. When Native Americans first saw European sailing ships, they had no experience adequate enough to understand what the ships were. They knew that these

---

[4]Understanding how persons develop in their religious and theological profiles has been the special concern of James W. Fowler. See *Stages of Faith: The Psychology of Human Development and the Quest for Meaning* (San Francisco: Harper & Row, 1984); *Becoming an Adult, Becoming Christian: Adult Development and Christian Faith* (San Francisco: Harper & Row, 1984); and *Stages of Faith and Religious Development* (New York: Crossroad, 1991). Compare this with the work of Lawrence Kohlberg, who has investigated how persons grow in moral sensibility. See *The Psychology of Moral Development: The Nature and Validity of Moral Stages* (San Francisco: Harper & Row, 1984).

strange objects on the water were obviously not canoes. Noting the ships' billowing sails, they figured out that these were a special kind of *cloud.*

We may smile, but in effect we do the same thing. Our usual response to something challenging is to "tame" it, to cut it down to our size. And even when we are intentionally open to the new, we can begin to understand it only in terms of what we already know. That's the natural human response.

But if we stay only within these responses, our capacity for reflective thinking remains at a primitive level. In this initial developmental stage, education only means encountering additional information with the assumption that it is either right or wrong. Instructors and authors are seen primarily as authorities presenting factual knowledge. And when we meet conflicting points of view, we tend to remain quiet until we come to know what we suppose is the right answer. Great numbers of people never get beyond this first stage. The reasons are several. Because much practical knowledge works along these lines, we tend to assume all knowledge does. In addition, many never have opportunities to encounter new ways of thinking. And others, even if exposed, never get beyond the anxiety that educational challenges pose.

But there is an important discovery that we can make that represents the first major development in thinking critically. Contrary to our initial sense that education means gaining more information, we can discover that the *assumptions* by which we understand something can be more important than *what* we know. Having insight does not consist merely of learning more subject matter. It means becoming aware of how we interpret the information we already have—like Native Americans did when they first saw European sailing ships.

In other words, understanding includes discovering that we see everything *from a particular perspective.* That is why I have drawn constant attention to the need to be aware of our unconscious assumptions in theology. This new stage of thinking also challenges us to recognize that not everyone shares our perspective or wants to. And as we begin to become aware of how perspectives operate for ourselves and others—including the books we read, the lectures we hear, and the authorities we appeal to—our sense of things begins to shift.

At first we are tempted to assume all perspectives but our own are "wrong." But gradually we are able to see that, in certain cases, the issue is not a matter of right or wrong. Sometimes differences are a reflection of respective limitations. Isaac Newton's theory of the universe isn't wrong, it's limited. He knew nothing about subatomic structures and the relativity of space and time. But that doesn't invalidate his careful analysis of the physical universe; it merely relativizes it. Within a certain context, Newton's physics is quite useful, as, for example, in guiding the principles of engineering. But it has *limited* usefulness. When we begin to see the limits of our own perspective and begin to share another, our potential for expanding our understanding increases.

One of my colleagues has a map that was posted on his office door for several years. It's a map of the Western hemisphere, but *South* America is depicted on the *top* and North America on the bottom. The caption, which is titled "A New World of Understanding," draws attention to the subtle way in which "above" and "below" have overtones of value and dominance. It also causes the viewer to begin to become aware of how these subtle connotations have applied to the way in which we North Americans have tended to see ourselves and our neighbors to the south. "This Turnabout Map of the Americas," it notes, "serves to correct the imbalance. It is geographically correct. Only the perspective has been changed." That's the point. The facts, the information, are the same, but the implicit assumptions are different. Seeing things in new perspective can literally make a world of difference. We learn to qualify and expand our understanding.

Throughout the preceding pages I have given many examples of changing and alternative perspectives and the effect this has on pursuing theology. It takes a while for us to become conscious of the assumptions we take for granted and the perspective from which we see things. We assume, like the world of common sense I referred to in chapter 3, that everyone has always thought about things this way. We *assume*, for example, that the most valid truth amounts to recognizing and demonstrating *facts*. It is a shock to discover that this assumption is not self-evident. It came about with the rise of modern science. There have been other types of knowing prior to this historical movement, and there have been qualifications of it since.

The point is, our way of understanding things is always limited. We cannot escape seeing the world of human experience from a particular perspective. Just as we are mortal, our understanding is always finite. As Paul puts it, "We know only in part, and we prophesy only in part" (1 Cor. 13:9). That doesn't necessarily invalidate what we believe. But it does qualify it and make clear that it is limited by definite operating assumptions.

The same holds true for the context of our knowing. What is valid in one situation or culture or historical period is invalid in another. The story is told of a giant who found a man unconscious and almost frozen in the snow. He brought him to his home, wrapped a blanket around him, and set him by the fire. The man came to and began to blow on his frozen fingers. The giant asked him what he was doing, and the man said he was trying to warm his hands. Then the giant brought him some piping hot soup to eat, whereupon the man began blowing on it. When the giant asked what he was doing, the man said he was trying to cool the soup. At this the giant angrily tossed him out into the cold again, since the man was obviously trying to make a fool of him by claiming his breath could both warm and cool something. The point of the story is that what makes something true has to do with its context.

This holds true for claims to religious truth. But it takes us a while to recognize and then legitimate any perspectives other than our own. None of this comes easily. Religious convictions are very dear to us; they are an important part of how we define ourselves—even if we are atheists! Because they mean so much to us, because they have to do with what we consider to be important and most deeply true, we resist any admission that other perspectives might have equal or more legitimacy than ours or that our dearest convictions reflect finite knowledge.

This transition is a difficult one for us to make. We need to recognize that from the very beginning. When such awareness first threatens to impact us, the tendency is to respond in a defensive way because it feels as if our deepest beliefs are under attack. In such a situation, we tend to seek reassurance by clustering with others who think like we do. Many times we are tempted to say little by way of direct response, since, for all our passion and conviction, we really aren't sure of ourselves. Instead, we dismiss alternative viewpoints from a safe distance. Instead of engaging directly in argument and open-ended reflection, we feel more comfortable with "our own kind" and are tempted to backbite and dismiss alternative points of view without giving them a fair hearing.

Some of us stay stuck at this point. But others of us undertake an act of spiritual courage. We dare to open ourselves up and reach out to what we don't yet understand. We begin to recognize that there are differing perspectives, that we all have operating assumptions that we take for granted even though they are not self-evident. And we also begin to tolerate perspectives that differ from our own. As that begins to happen, however, we face a new set of challenges.

Learning to Make Judgments and Cases

A fair number of college-educated people make the transition to the second stage of critical thinking. They recognize that we all see issues from our own perspectives and are willing to recognize a plurality of views. They see the qualified nature of all outlooks, beliefs, and convictions. Instead of coarsely insisting, "This, that, or the next thing is so!" they knowingly sprinkle their assertions with the phrase "It seems to me that…" And they display a growing ability to enter into others' viewpoints. This enables them to expand or at least qualify their own.

If this doesn't describe you yet, it may if you give yourself time and are willing to enter the process. And in facing the possibility of this transition, you will have to learn to "depersonalize" the probing questions that are leveled at your assumptions. They may feel like personal attacks, but they are not. They are a summons for you to discover the truth about yourself and the world more deeply than you already have. As I've indicated before, believing Christians should be more ready to make this transition because trust in God means the willingness to give up illusions of mastery and control. If you yourself are a serious Christian, think about it, and I'm bold enough to add, pray about it.

But there are two major hurdles people face once they admit that there's no escape from delimitation and pluralism. First, they find it hard to make comparisons between different points of view; and second, they find it hard to back up their own assertions. The result is often an easy-going—even indifferent—tolerance and a reluctance or inability to affirm any convictions. The easiest response is either to go along with the views of the instructor without questioning them or to allow all sorts of ideas to germinate indiscriminately. "Let a hundred flowers bloom; let a thousand thoughts contend," wrote Mao Tse-Tung.

Students of theology who are fixed in this stage are constantly frustrated when, in response to written papers or exams or comments in class, they are told, in effect, "Make a *case*, not just an assertion!" They don't know how. And they don't think it is necessary. After all, they assume, theology deals with what amounts to private opinions. And because what a person believes is his or her own affair, and since no one should tell another what to believe, one opinion is as good as another. Opinions cannot be evaluated; they can only be shared.

This echoes the interview with a young nurse given the pseudonym "Sheila Larson" in a now-famous probing study of American religion. She described her own expression of religion by referring to a belief in God, but one that was generally devoid of any content and didn't go beyond her sense of her self very much. "My faith has carried me a long way," she observed. "It's Sheilaism. Just my own little voice."[5] And,

---

[5] Robert N. Bellah, et al., *Habits of the Heart: Individualism and Commitment in American Life* (New York: Harper & Row, 1985), 221. Additional reflections on "Sheilaism" are found on page 235.

of course, the implication is that if this is all we can say, if we are ultimately reduced to a religious truth that is solely subjective, then by rights we should have over two hundred million different religions here in the United States!

Certainly, indoctrination and intimidation are unworthy both of the gospel and of the process of education. No one should be coerced into accepting religious doctrine. But if tolerant plurality only amounts to personal opinion, then we should disband the Christian church and education as well. Yes, we always see *in part*, but we look at a *shared* world. Luther once said that the individual soul and God no more need a third party than a husband and wife. But the God who is God is never our own private deity. When students responded to his academic challenges by replying, in effect, "That's only *your* reality," a former colleague of mine had a telling comeback. He always asked, "Why bother to tell me about it, then?" If we are locked into ourselves, then there can be no shared life, no communication. And anything goes—even Charles Manson and Adolf Hitler.

Perhaps we will grow to see the limits and context of our own perspective and be willing to enter into the perspectives of others. But achieving this does not relieve us of the need to make judgments. There is more than private opinion at stake. Certainly this is true for those who claim to be Christians and part of a community of belief. But it is true in the academic and public arenas as well. Not every assertion is of equal value, even if it is argued sincerely and with great passion. Often people are tempted to credit anything asserted with sincerity and deep feeling. But it's not enough. All sorts of political and religious fanatics have sincerely meant what they said. But firmness of belief is no proof of validity—or even of sanity.

What, then, are the criteria of assertions that can be argued as being better than others? The first is that they are more informed. They have more complete and accurate information. Some theology is more *knowledgeable* than the rest. No one can know or has known everything. But some persons are better informed than others. That's why I suggest that the best place to begin theological study is in getting acquainted with the catholic tradition—from its biblical roots to the present. You can be better informed than you are now. A second criterion for *Christian* theology (and which for Christians should have first priority) is an elaboration of the first: Theology needs to present clear arguments about why it believes it is being *faithful* to the foundations of the church's faith and life in Jesus Christ. Christian theology aims at *normative* statements, not private ones. Therefore, it needs to express why it claims to be authentically Christian and not merely a matter of private opinion.

A third criterion that can justify some theology as better than others is that it is more *inclusive,* more comprehensive in its scope. It ties together and integrates relevant material better, even if no totally comprehensive system of theology is possible. For example, a theology that treats the doctrine of God by sympathetically understanding and then responding to atheistic criticisms is better than a theology that ignores them. That can cause beginning theology students problems because one of the technical aspects of writing in theology is authors' goal of coming to grips with relevant issues. That's why they resort to the "theological shorthand" noted in chapter 3. A fourth and related criterion is that better theology is theology that is *illuminating,* if we can put it this way. This is the most elusive criterion, but it is perhaps one of the most important. Theology is more valid if it opens up Christian faith and life to people in a way that enables them to sense greater measures of relevance and deeper reaches of personal impact. Theology can rightly claim authority if it helps us see more deeply and widely into ourselves, the larger world in which we live, and the richness of God.

A fifth criterion is that one theological position has more validity than others if it is more *coherent,* that is, more consistent in its arguments. This means making a careful argument that demonstrates how various assertions exhibit an internal consistency. It also means not violating the patterns of logic in making arguments. And, parenthetically, better theology doesn't use poor arguments to support good conclusions.

Two final criteria that show the transition from the first to the second stage of critical thinking. The first is that better theology is theology that is *self-conscious* about its own particular context and origins. It is theology that admits it speaks out of a particular place and time and is shaped by the concerns and even personal history of the theologian. Admitting these limits and then exploring them and their value is better than not seeing them at all. Accordingly, better theology demonstrates awareness of its operating presuppositions and presents arguments for them. This includes putting one's hermeneutical cards on the table, being conscious of one's method, and being willing to let these assumptions be scrutinized and critiqued by one's theological peers.

And a related criterion at this point is that better theology is more *permeable,* as someone has put it. It's more open to alternatives and is willing to learn from them. It can play "devil's advocate" with itself by trying to understand alternatives and criticisms as well as possible and then responding to them. It tries to be intellectually fair by representing alternative points of view as carefully as possible. The best test of this is the capacity to cite an opposing view to the satisfaction of those who hold it.

None of these criteria enable us to step out of our own skins or avoid our own limits. But they enable us to make discriminating judgments within them. We do not have to settle for endless numbers of subjective opinions that coexist alongside of each other with no basis for conversation, mutual criticism, or cross-fertilization. We may not have a handle on "absolute" truth, but we can discover some points of view that *are relatively better* than others.

Working with these criteria, we can learn to make a theological *case* and not simply theological assertions. We can begin to give *reasons* for our affirmations. Recognizing and responding to criteria of judgment is as hard for persons at the second stage as understanding the roles of "perspectives" and "assumptions" is for persons in the first. But just as one can discover and respond to the latter, one can also do so with the former.

There are still two more stages of developing critical thinking beyond that of discovering the capacity for judgments. I won't elaborate them, since they probably aren't relevant to you right now. But perhaps it will help to know that they exist. The first is the recognition that once we learn to make reasoned cases, even the best arguments are limited. One can give reasons, but they are never exhaustive or absolute. As I've noted, some theological affirmations are better than others, but they are only *relatively* better, not absolutely so.

It's not just beginning students of theology who can get stuck here but professors as well. There are some who, in the course of advanced studies, find that they have no absolute ground on which to stand, so they don't believe they can stand for very much of anything. All that is left to them is the honesty of radical self-criticism, the undermining of all absolute and unqualified claims, and the unstinting humility about the limits of everything. For such persons, theology can be a rigorous academic pursuit, but it tends to be devoid of personal commitment.

I can remember my first years of graduate studies in theology at what all understood to be a high-pressure institution. How I scrambled. Everywhere I turned, I discovered my ignorance. I was intimidated by the fact that others seemed to know so much more than I did. And of course I assumed that my own knowledge and experience were common to everyone, so that it didn't count for much. I had my own theological perspective but believed it couldn't stand the test of the intense rigor of analysis that went on and therefore kept a low profile. But, gradually, I made two very important discoveries.

The first was that everyone else was in the same predicament to a greater or lesser degree. Certainly, they had background and comprehension about all sorts of things that I didn't have, but the reverse was also true. I had some insights that few others shared. I also discovered that if we became caught up in the game of professional one-up-person-ship, then our anxieties about the limits of our understanding prevented us from being totally open. That in turn kept us from supporting one another and being resources for each other. It also became apparent that our own anxieties kept us from really saying what we believed because we could never substantiate it exhaustively. Our convictions were *never* beyond criticism or controversy. And so, too often we sat with our cards held close to our chests, not daring to let others know what we believed and thereby expose our naiveté.

But developmental psychology says that there is yet another stage toward which the educational process can lead us, one that encourages us to embrace our convictions even while recognizing both our limits and our inability to cover all the critical bases. We learn how to make confessional affirmations in a context of spirited and open dialogue with other points of view. We recognize the importance and the validity of our own testimony in this context. Others can learn from us, but this requires us to represent our perspective as faithfully and as carefully as we can. At the same time, we are open to learn from them. To use a phrase coined by Martin Marty, this phase of critical thinking expresses "convinced openness." I believe that this is coherent with what the author of Ephesians had in mind in referring to "speaking the truth in love" (Eph. 4:15).

In this situation, conviction has not disappeared, even though it is now qualified and humbled. Knowledge learned from others is integrated with the inner truth of experience and personal reflection. Knower and known become intimately intertwined and exist in a consciously recognized historical and cultural context. Theology consciously takes up the task of speaking as *faithful* a word as it can, "a word spoken in season," even while acknowledging that it cannot speak a *final* word. After all, that is the call that the prophets and apostles experienced. They spoke in and for their own times and places, and yet, interestingly, *because of* this—not in spite of it—their words and witness continue to enrich and challenge persons in other times and other places. That is how "insight" operates. It isn't "absolute," that is, it isn't "absolved" from the limitations of culture and history.

Instead, it has the capacity to speak a rich word that can transcend these limitations.

Summary

- The value of "a gyroscopic center" and the inadequacy of contemporary catechesis suggest that theological study best begins with coming to know the broad tradition of catholic doctrine and specific church traditions.

- Deep understanding of a major theologian or particular theological "school" may also provide concrete orientation in the current situation of theological pluralism, as long as the wider setting is appreciated.

- Because it is possible for us to grow intellectually, emotionally, and spiritually, we may discover that we can grow to appreciate theological perspectives that earlier confused or intimidated us.

- According to developmental psychology, critical thinking is a skill that can be learned and that enables persons increasingly to discover and accept the complexities of the world and the qualified nature of all understanding.

- The first transition in critical thinking entails moving beyond our assumption that every issue is a matter of right or wrong toward an increasing recognition of the role of unconscious assumptions and delimited contexts. The discovery of these perspectives can increase our capacity for sympathetic understanding.

- The second transition is from an indiscriminate acceptance of a plurality of perspectives and personal opinions to recognition of the criteria for making relative judgments. These criteria include greater measures of comprehensiveness, coherence, living meaningfulness, self-qualification, and permeability.

- Additional transitions include recognizing the relative character of such rational judgments and the willingness to embrace this relativity in "convinced openness."

For Further Reading and Reflection

There are two significant problems in identifying texts in systematic theology for beginning students. The first is finding titles that are theologically substantive and that at the same time are written in a clear style and at an introductory level. The second is the fact that, due to federal tax laws, publishing companies do not keep large inventories and consequently, apart from consistent best sellers, do not reprint books or have them in their inventories for very long. Therefore, once a helpful text appears, it is only available for a short while. Many of the titles given below are out of print but should be available in theological libraries.

Baly, Denis, and Royal W. Rhodes. *The Faith of Christians: An Introduction to Basic Beliefs.* Philadelphia: Fortress Press, 1984. A book written by two college professors who developed a course addressing the fact that "ordinary people in this country are often startlingly ignorant of even the elements of the Christian faith" and then incorporated the responses of the twenty students who first took the course. Very readable.

Carmody, Denise L. *Christian Feminist Theology: A Constructive Interpretation.* Oxford/Cambridge, Mass.: Blackwell, 1995. As the title indicates, this is a systematic theology that, as the book cover notes, is "indebted to both traditional Christian faith and recent feminist thought critical of that faith." Carmody writes with a very lucid, even lyrical, style and is accessible to the beginning student of theology.

Evans, Alice F., and Robert A. Evans. *Introduction to Christianity: A Case Method Approach.* Atlanta: John Knox Press, 1980. A novel approach to Christian doctrine that shows its relevance in regard to specific case studies.

Fackre, Dorothy, and Gabriel Fackre. *Christian Basics: A Primer for Pilgrims.* Grand Rapids: Eerdmans, 1991. Approaches theology as a narrative story and includes helpful diagrams, a glossary of terms, and reflection questions. Basic catechesis.

Ferner, Johannes, and Lukas Vischer, eds. *A Common Catechism: A Book of Christian Faith.* New York: Seabury Press, 1975.

The English translation of a catechism jointly produced for adult instruction by German Roman Catholics and Protestants.

Gratsch, Edward J., ed. *Principles of Catholic Theology*. New York: Alba House, 1981. Several Roman Catholic theologians cooperated in producing this nontechnical overview of contemporary teaching in that tradition.

Jersild, Paul. *Invitation to Faith: Christian Belief Today*. Minneapolis: Augsburg Publishing, 1978. Very readable and substantive overview. Unfortunately out of print but worth searching down.

Neville, Robert C. A *Theology Primer*. Albany: State University of New York Press, 1991. A fresh approach to traditional doctrines that is conversant with contemporary philosophy. Chapters end with references for further reading in major classical and contemporary theologians. Neville's style borders on "academese," but concentration will catch his meaning.

For more advanced one-volume discussions of basic Christian doctrine, note the following possibilities:

Bloesch, Donald. *Essentials of Evangelical Theology*. San Francisco: Harper & Row, 1979. An evangelical conservative in the Reformed tradition updates classical doctrines.

Cauthen, Kenneth. *Systematic Theology: A Modern Protestant Approach*. Lewiston, N.Y.: Edward Mellen Press, 1986. A very readable, helpful panoramic survey of contemporary theology. Unfortunately, very expensive.

Evans, Robert A., and Thomas D. Parker, eds. *Christian Theology: A Case Study Approach*. New York: Harper and Row, 1976. A novel approach to theology in which case studies are presented and then commented on by leading ecumenical theologians.

Fiorenza, Francis Schüssler, and John P. Galvin. *Systematic Theology: Roman Catholic Perspectives*. As the title indicates, this is a treatment of major doctrines by leading English-speaking Roman Catholic theologians.

Gilkey, Langdon. *Message and Existence: An Introduction to Christian Theology*. New York: Seabury Press, 1981. One of the prominent American Protestant theologians shows the interrelationship of divine revelation and human experience in the theological tradition of Paul Tillich.

Hall, Douglas John. *Professing the Faith: Christian Theology in a North American Context*. Minneapolis: Fortress Press, 1993. The second of a three-volume project. Hall provides an insightful analysis of the present cultural context and its implications for church life and theology.

Hodgson, Peter C., and Robert H. King. *Christian Theology: An Introduction to its Traditions and Tasks*, revised and enlarged ed. Philadelphia: Fortress Press, 1985. Treatment of classical *loci* by leading ecumenical theologians.

Hodgson, Peter C. and Robert H. King, eds. *Readings in Christian Theology*. Philadelphia: Fortress Press, 1985. A companion volume to the one noted above that provides readings from classical and contemporary theologians of many traditions.

Jenson, Robert W. *Story and Promise*. Mifflintown, Penn.: Sigler Press, 1989. A reprint of a theology shaped by metachronics. The gospel is the unique *story* of Jesus as it is being worked out in personal and corporate history as its *promise* moves toward a final fulfillment.

LaCugna, Catherine Mowry, ed. *Freeing Theology: The Essentials of Theology in Feminist Perspective*. New York: HarperCollins, 1993. A highly stimulating study of major *loci* by ten Roman Catholic theologians who, while remaining grounded in tradition, have been deeply influenced by feminist insight and concerns.

Ratzinger, Joseph. *Introduction to Christianity*. New York: Seabury Press, 1979. A reflection of the impact of the Second Vatican Council in opening up Roman Catholic teaching to the modern world by someone who is now a traditionalist cardinal resisting liberal tendencies in that community.

Song, Choan-Seng. *Third Eye Theology: A Theology in Formation in Asian Settings*. Maryknoll, N.Y.: Orbis Books, 1979. A totally novel approach to Christian theology by a leading Asian theologian who reflects non-Western ways of thinking.

Suchocki, Marjorie. *God. Christ. Church: A Practical Guide to Process Theology*. New York: Crossroad, 1987. As the subtitle indicates, a treatment of classical doctrinal themes with process and feminist sensitivities.

Wainwright, Geoffrey. *Doxology: The Praise of God in Worship. Doctrine and Life: A Systematic Theology.* New York: Oxford University Press, 1980. An English Methodist links theology to the widest reaches of church life.

After mastering introductory and more advanced studies in Christian doctrine, you will be ready to tackle the work of influential theologians. These would include the "giants" of mid-century, such as Karl Barth, Paul Tillich, and Karl Rahner, but also contemporary figures (to name only a few—in alphabetical order), such as John B. Cobb, Jr., Edward Farley, Gustavo Gutierrez, Kosuke Koyama, Hans Küng, Sallie McFague, John Macquarrie, John Mbiti, Jurgen Moltmann, Wolfhart Pannenberg, Rosemary Radford Ruether, Jon Sobrino, and David Tracy.

To gain a panoramic view of issues and options in contemporary theology, note the following:

Ferm, Dean William. *Contemporary American Theologies: A Critical Survey.* New York: Seabury Press, 1981. A helpful review of the recent history of American theology and summary of a number of important movements including evangelical conservatism, feminist, and African American.

———. *3rd World Liberation Theologies: An Introductory Survey.* Maryknoll, N.Y.: Orbis Books, 1986. A helpful survey.

Ford, David, ed. *The Modern Theologians: An Introduction to Christian Theology in the Twentieth Century,* 2d ed. Cambridge, Mass.: Blackwell, 1997. As the subtitle indicates, this is a panoramic survey of significant theologians and trends up to the present.

Hordern, William E. *A Layman's Guide to Protestant Theology,* revised and expanded ed. New York: Macmillan, 1968. A highly readable and informative overview of the major theological options at the middle of this century, limited only by not being updated and reprinted.

Kliever, Lonnie D. *The Shattered Spectrum: A Survey of Contemporary Theology.* Atlanta: John Knox Press, 1981. Although dated, most of the theological trends treated in this book have played important roles in shaping subsequent theology right to the present.

Küng, Hans, and David Tracy. *Paradigm Change in Theology.* This is a very advanced book written by a number of leading contemporary ecumenical theologians exploring a "postmodern" situation.

Macquarrie, John. *Twentieth Century Religious Thought: The Frontiers of Philosophy and Theology. 1900-1960.* New York: Harper and Row, 1963. The title says it all. Thorough, careful but demanding style and content.

Peerman, Dean. *Frontline Theology.* Richmond, Va.: John Knox Press, 1967. A collection of brief essays describing the influences that shaped them and the conscious aims that claim them by eighteen leading mid-century North American Protestant and Roman Catholic theologians.

Pinnock, Clark. *Tracking the Maze.* San Francisco: Harper & Row, 1990. The subtitle captures the concerns of this book—"finding our way through modern theology from [a conservative] evangelical perspective."

Viladesau, Richard, and Mark Massa. *Foundations of Theological Study: A Sourcebook.* New York/Mahwah, N.J.: Paulist Press, 1991. Two Roman Catholics provide an overview of ecumenical theology from the special perspective of that community.

Wall, James M., ed. *Theologians in Transition.* New York: Crossroad, 1981. This is a collection of essays written by twenty-one prominent theologians for a series titled "How My Mind Has Changed," which appeared in the journal *The Christian Century.*

Weaver, Mary Jo. *Introduction to Christianity.* Belmont, Calif.: Wadsworth, 1991. Designed for college courses in religion, this broadly focused book reviews the history of Christian life and thought up into the present.

Postscript

Theology is a journey that occurs on many levels. It entails being introduced to an extensive body of material that has a venerable history. You will have to gauge just how deeply you want or need to become acquainted with these materials. There are the many doctrines of the Christian community that have biblical roots and that have developed in subsequent centuries. There are important theological controversies that have been faced by the churches. Some have resulted in broad ecumenical consensus, some have yet to be resolved. There are technical terms whose definitions you need to discover. There are divergent approaches and arguments that have been going on for some time that you will stumble across without realizing and need to recognize. There is an extensive plurality of theology today that calls for your attention.

But for most persons, studying theology is more than entering into an academic discipline like any other. Most who are drawn to it are members of the Christian community to one degree or another and are personally involved. Therefore, there are deep emotional overtones, since academic issues impinge on personal beliefs and loyalties and issues of identity. Sometimes this can hamper our willingness to be open to critical study, which asks us to maximize our intellectual honesty, entertain radical questions, and become aware of our heretofore unquestioned assumptions. To do that requires more than mental exertion in mastering content. It requires a spiritual attitude of openness and courage.

At the deepest levels, theological study is a "rite of passage." In other words, it provides opportunities for us to change in directions of greater personal maturity. But as Christian psychoanalyst Scott Peck[1] points out, the sad truth about human beings is that we are inveterately sinful. And for Peck, sin is "spiritual laziness," deep resistance to change. We don't want to endure the dislocation and anxiety that comes with leaving the security of established opinions and patterns and risking ourselves through questioning and exposure to the new or different. That is the deepest challenge of theological study. Theology is more than learning additional information or developing new skills in discovering presuppositions or making rational arguments. It is an invitation to a spiritual journey that asks us to risk ourselves, to be willing to grow, to abandon our tendencies to reduce life to our own size, and to adopt strategies of control.

But if Peck is right, if resistance to growth is deeply entrenched in each one of us, what can encourage us to embrace risk? I believe we only dare to risk if we sense that ultimately we will also find support.

In introducing seminarians to theological study, recognizing their deep personal investment in their understanding of Christian faith and life, I make each of them a promise. My promise is, if you dare to risk yourself in facing the new and the alien, if you dare to let radical and probing questions challenge you, nothing of what you most deeply treasure will be lost. Your life in Christ, I tell them, will not suffer. Instead, I promise them, you will have it more richly and fully than ever. Your own religious profile might be quite different from theirs. You may be studying theology without any deep personal religious commitment, perhaps none at all, so little or nothing of what I am saying here may apply to you. But it may, if you are a believing Christian whose implicit theology has not been examined and tested.

The reason I can make that promise to Christian students of theology is that I don't have to keep it. That's the best sort

---

[1] M. Scott Peck, *The Road Less Traveled: A New Psychology of Love, Traditional Values, and Spiritual Growth* (New York: Simon and Schuster, 1978), esp. 271–79.

of promise to make! I don't stand behind that promise; I believe God's Spirit does. If Christians really trust God rather than their own convictions and emotional certainties, then they should be able to risk this rite of passage and find that it is yet one more way God can and will bless them.

So, having been introduced to the building blocks of theology, perhaps you are now ready to begin your studies. I wish you well and hope along the way that you, too, like Augustine and Aquinas, Calvin and Tillich, and so many others, will discover that at its very heart lies the invitation to *love* God—with all your mind.

www.ingramcontent.com/pod-product-compliance
Lightning Source LLC
Chambersburg PA
CBHW071435160426
43195CB00013B/1906